Throughout time man has admired the fleeting moments of exquisiteness and in his efforts to capture those moments he has painted upon thousands of canvas the innocence of beauty that he sees. Virtually in an effort to capture the very essence of life as it flows through time he has translated what he sees into vibrant colors to stimulate all the senses of ones own being. In sharp contrast an artist may choose conflicting lines to portray the starkness between day and night.

This book Art L'Amour Sensuel illustrates some of the greatest art work by master artists such as Pierre-Auguste Renoir as depicted on the cover, painted to recreate the splendor and beauty of the female body, heart and mind. Within this book is art that spans over hundreds of years and has brought the world the humblest of creations, yet so inflexible to paint and master. Art L'Amour Sensuel is devoted to those in the art world that recognize the creation of beauty, the simplest of moments, beginning of life which all civilizations around the world highly prize.

Welcome to

Art L'Amour Sensuel

The Masters Collection of art.

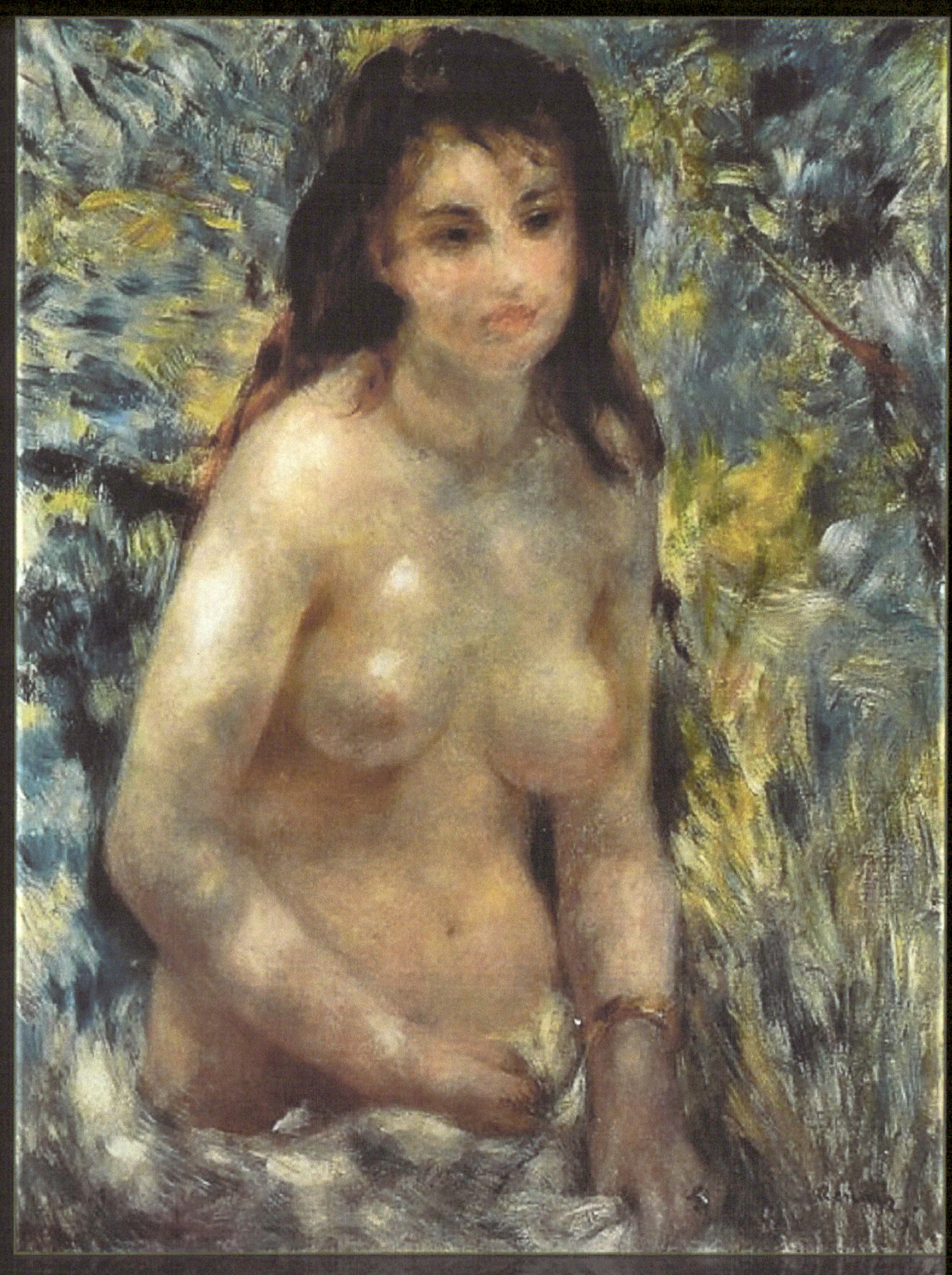

Pierre-Auguste Renoir - Torse, effet de soleil

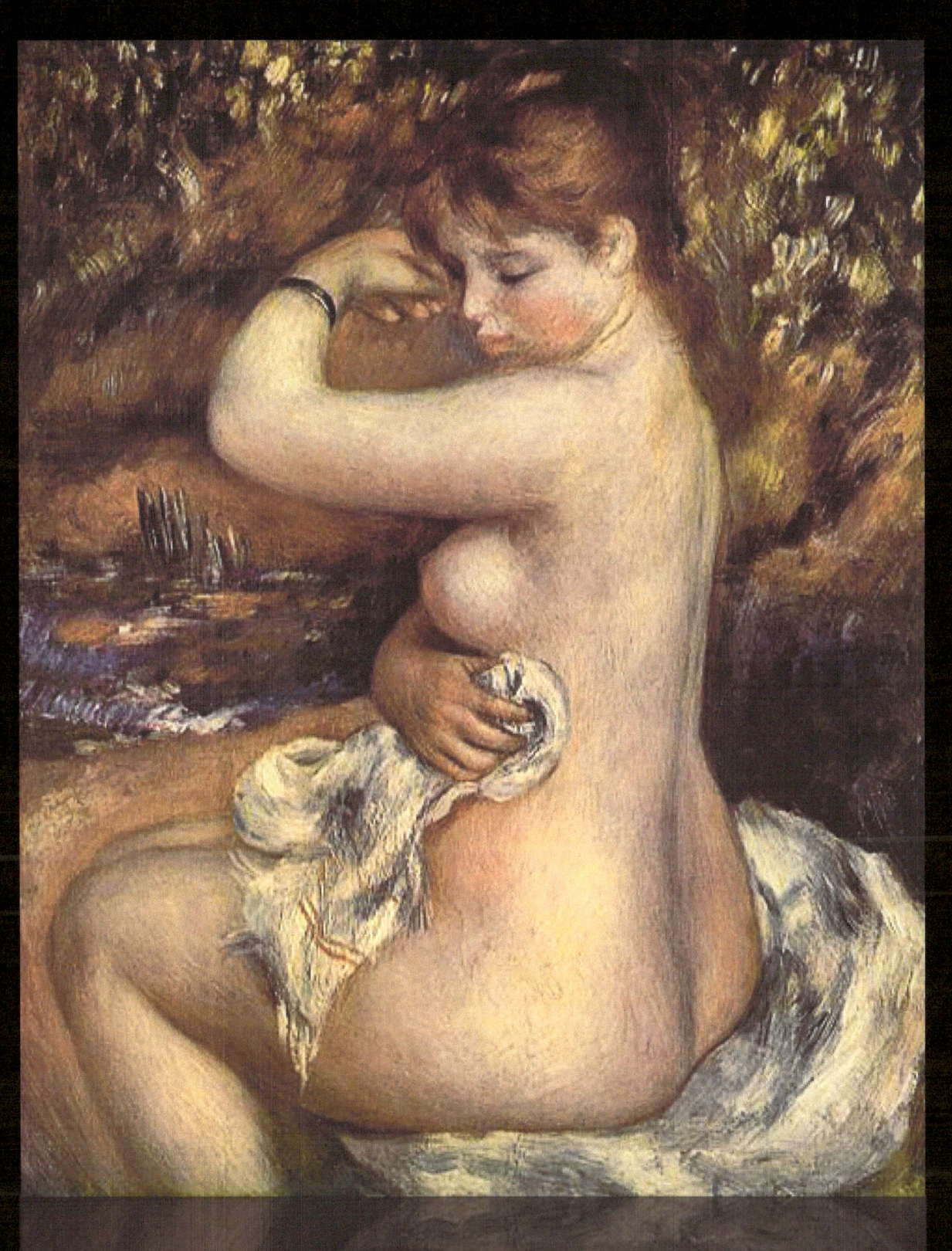

Pierre-Auguste Renoir - Torse, effet de soleil

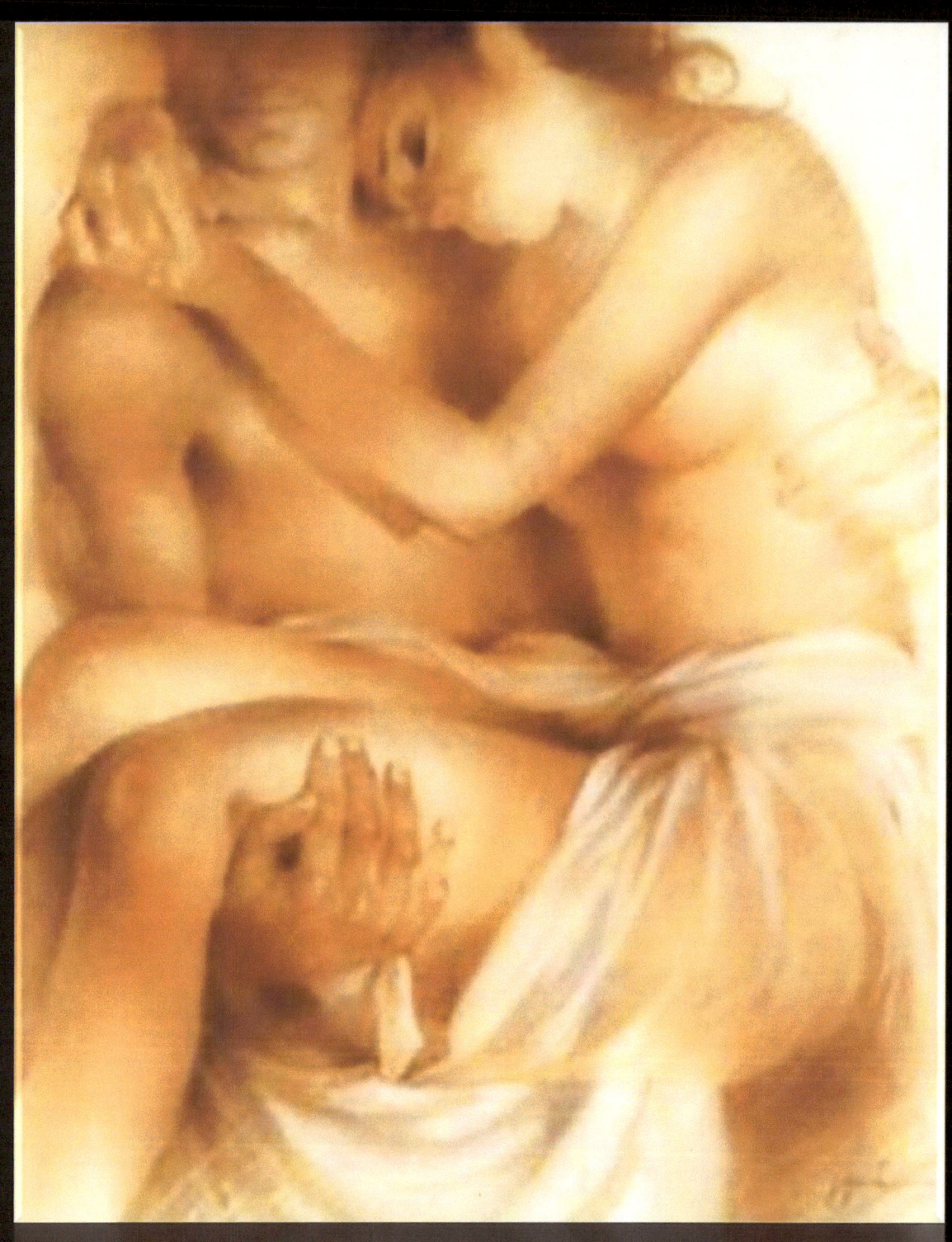

En Brazos De Morfeo Artist: Jose Aguilar

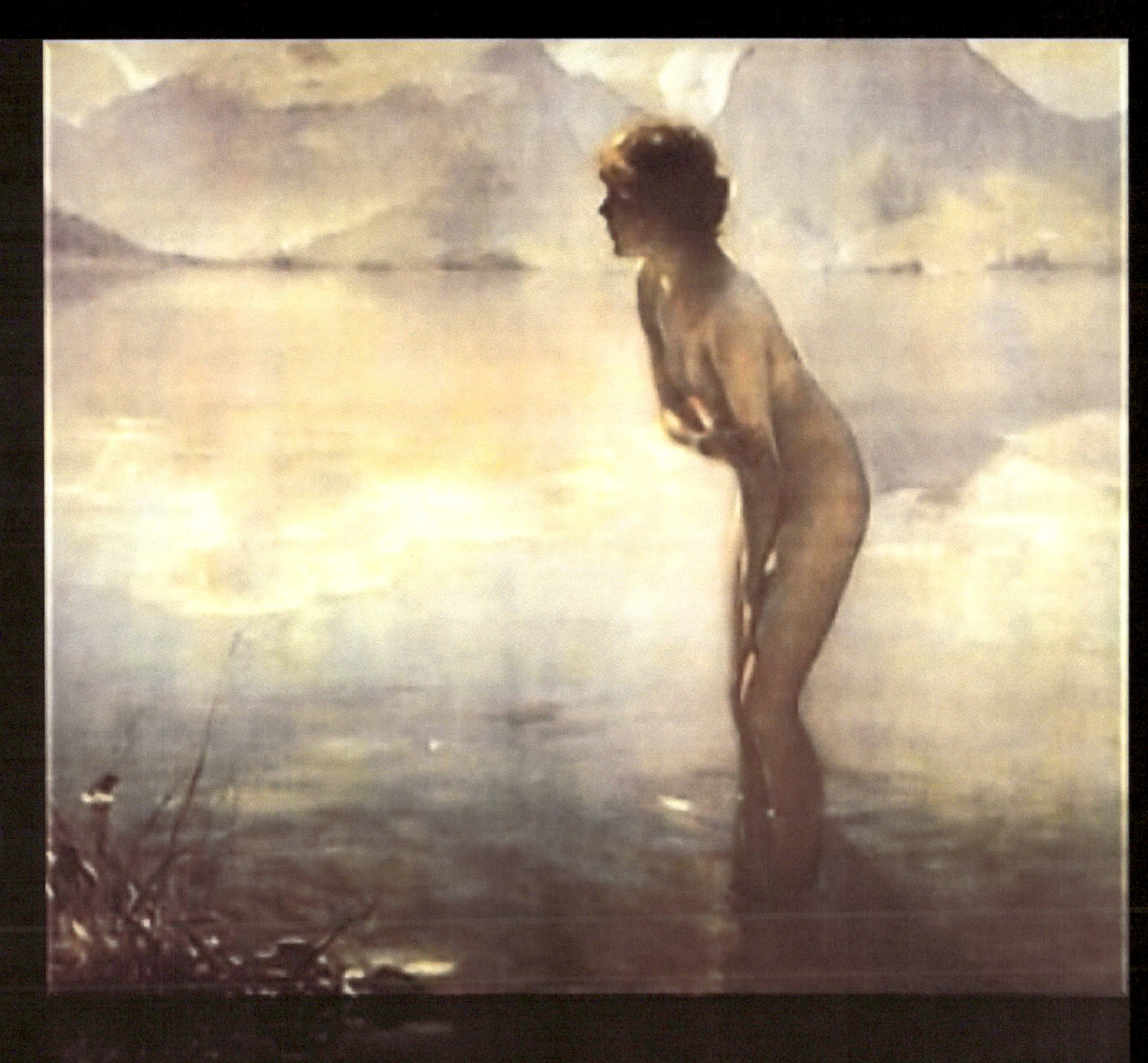

September Morn Paul Émile Chabas, 1869–1937

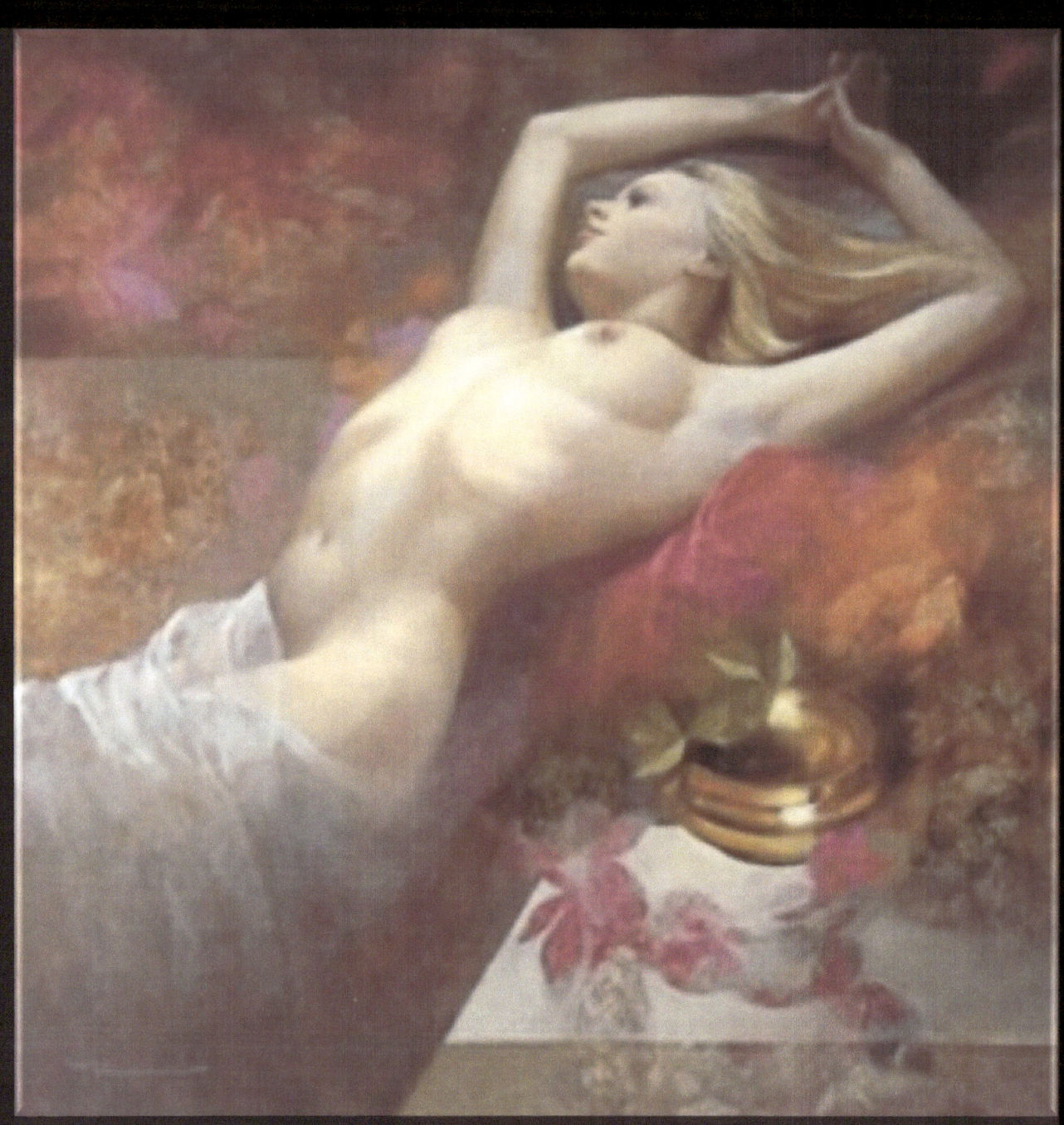

Golden dreams
Spartaco Lombardo

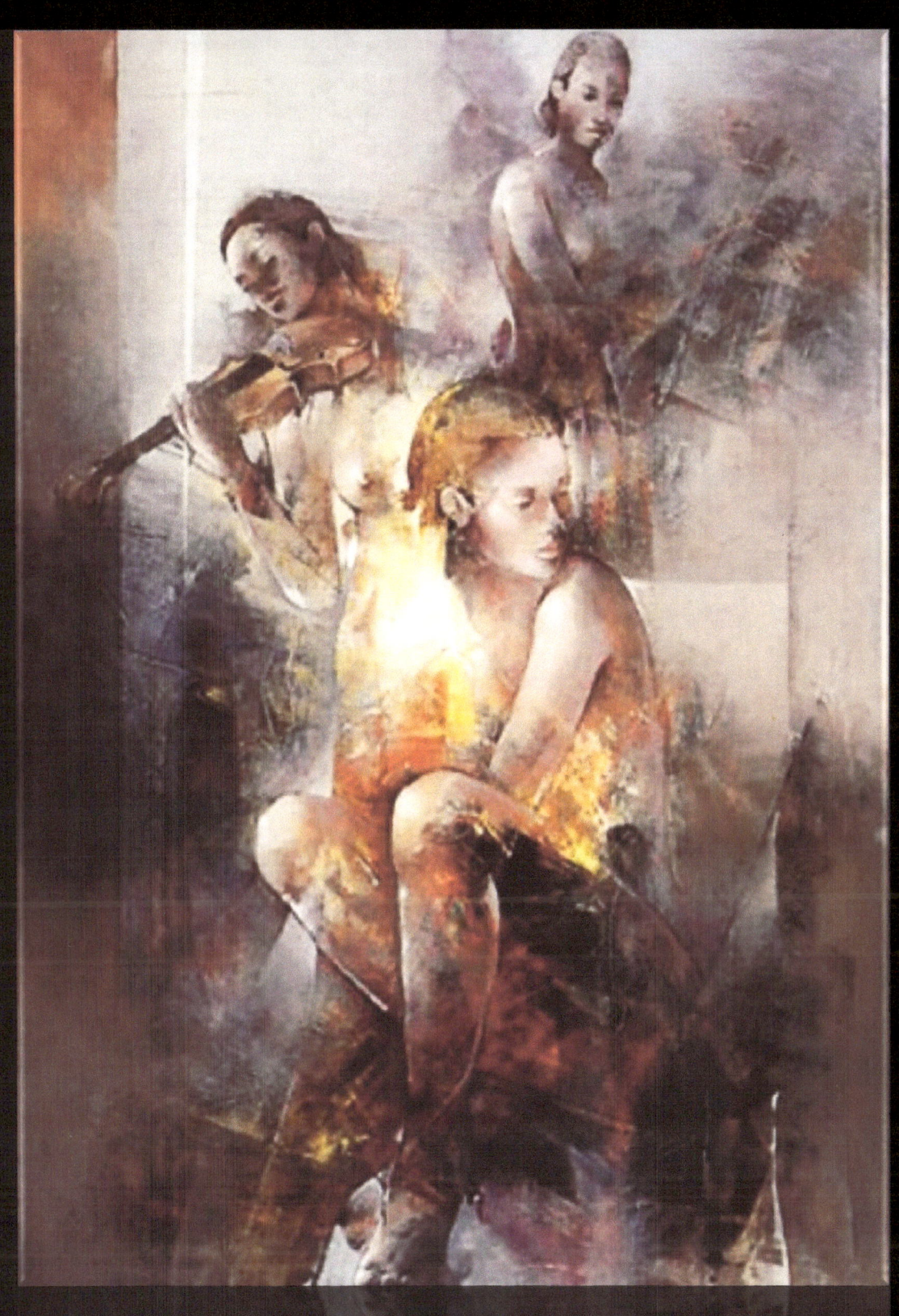

Prelude Nadia Cascini

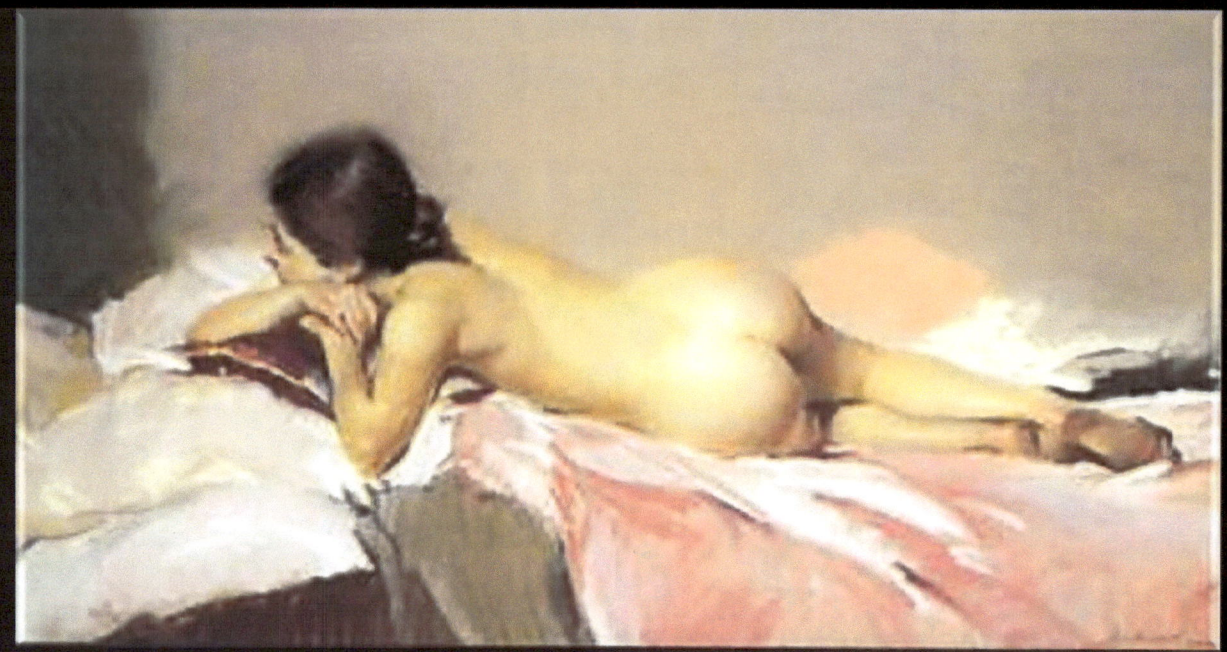

Nude on Pink Satin, Artist: <u>*Santamans*</u>

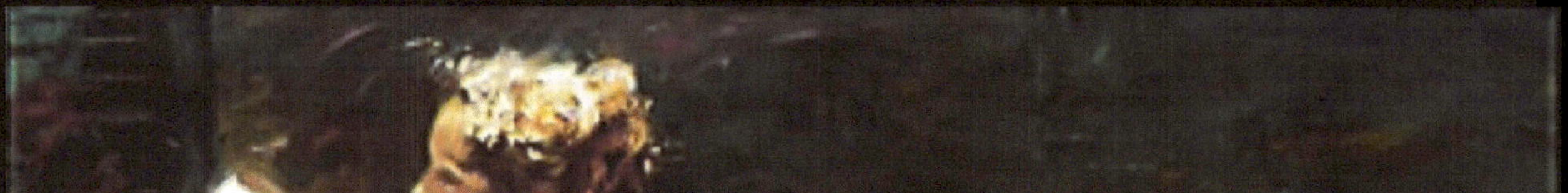

<u>*PinoEvening Repose*</u>

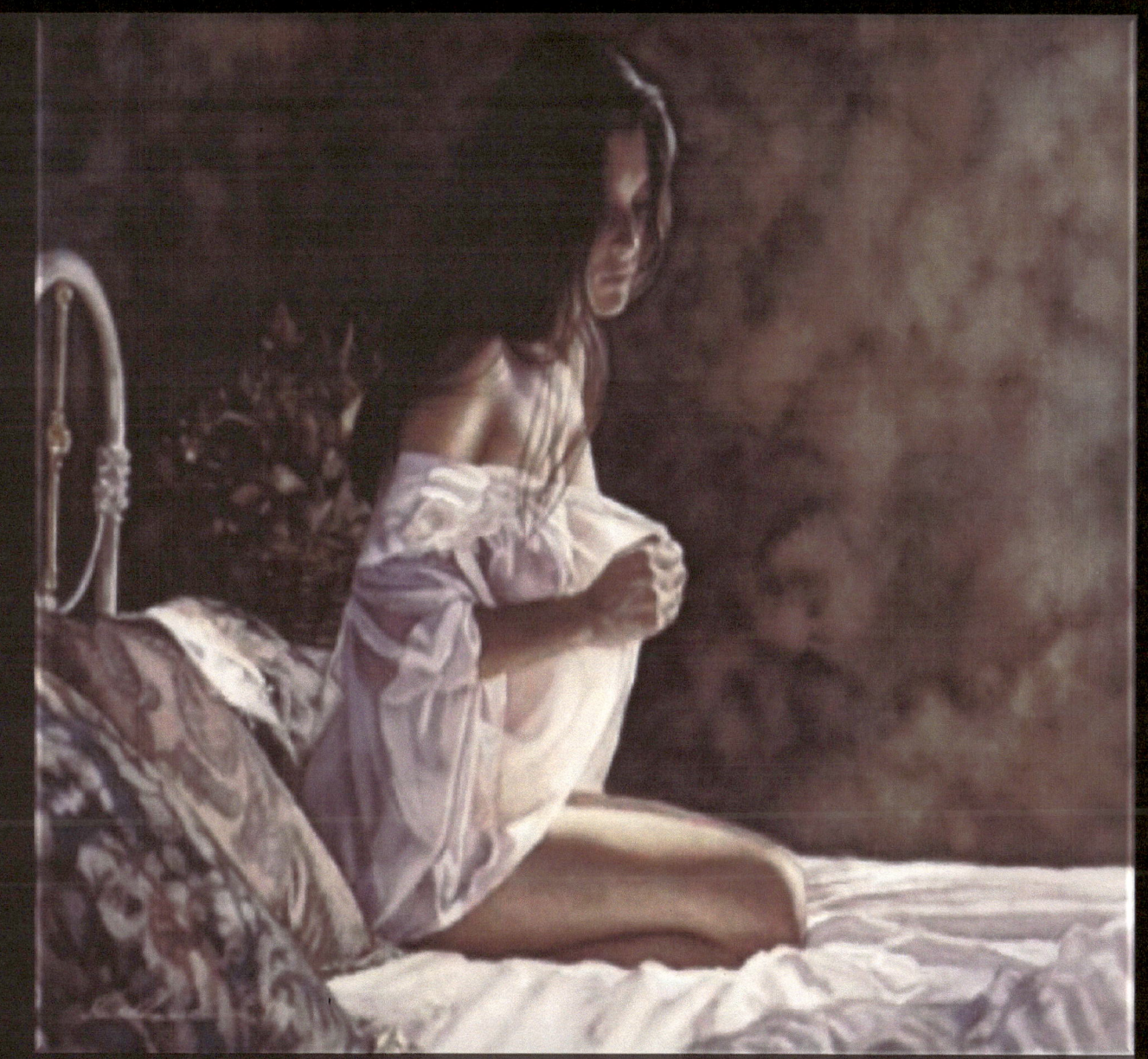

OW Second Thoughts by Steve Hanks

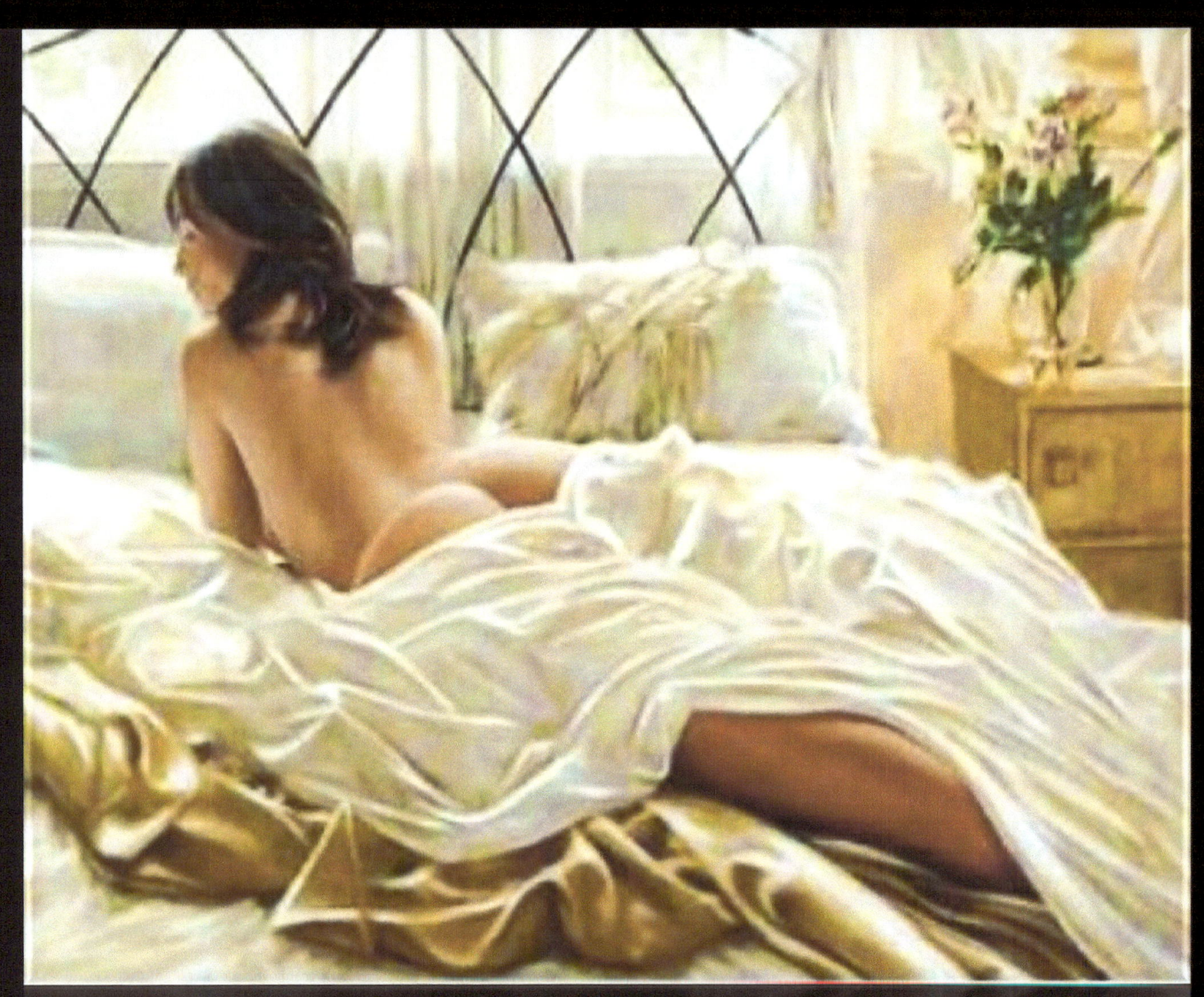

Chambre Estivale by Rob Hefferan

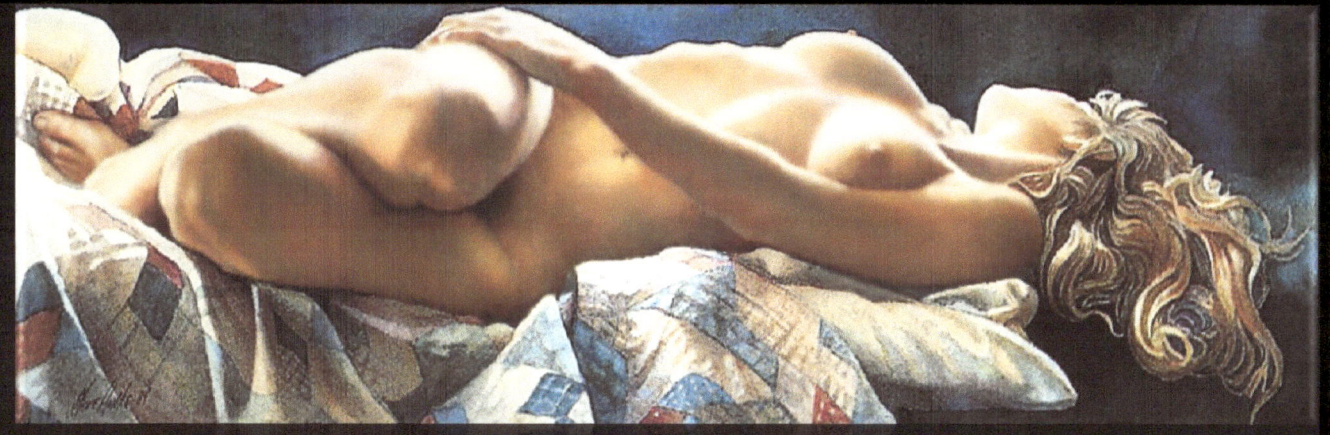

Reclining Nude<u>Steve Hanks</u>

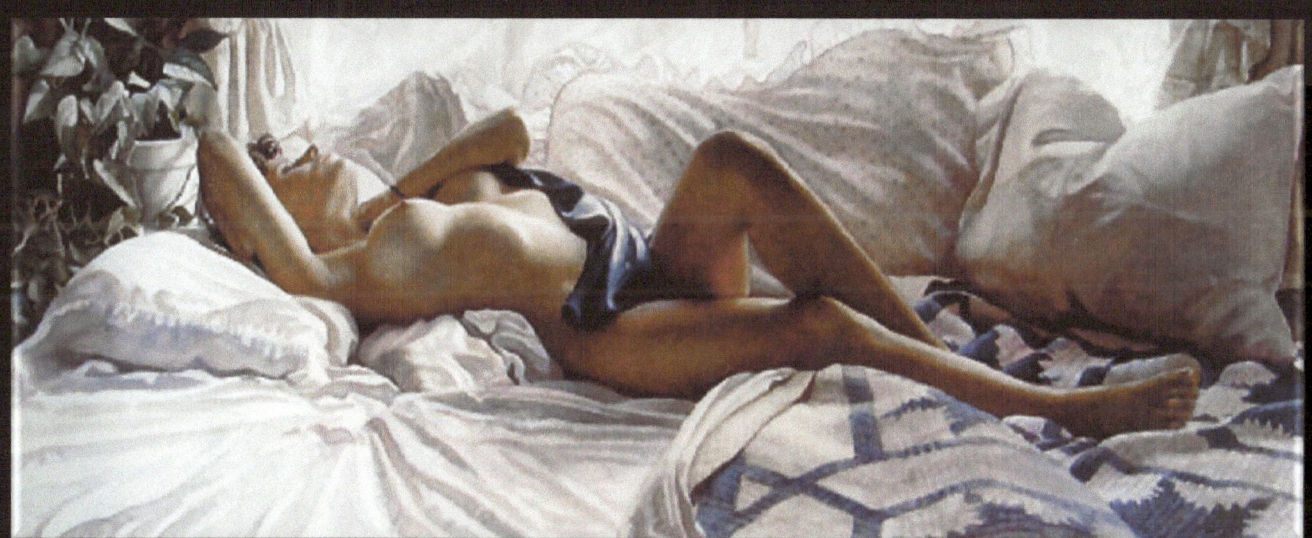

Steve Hanks Lost in the Reverie

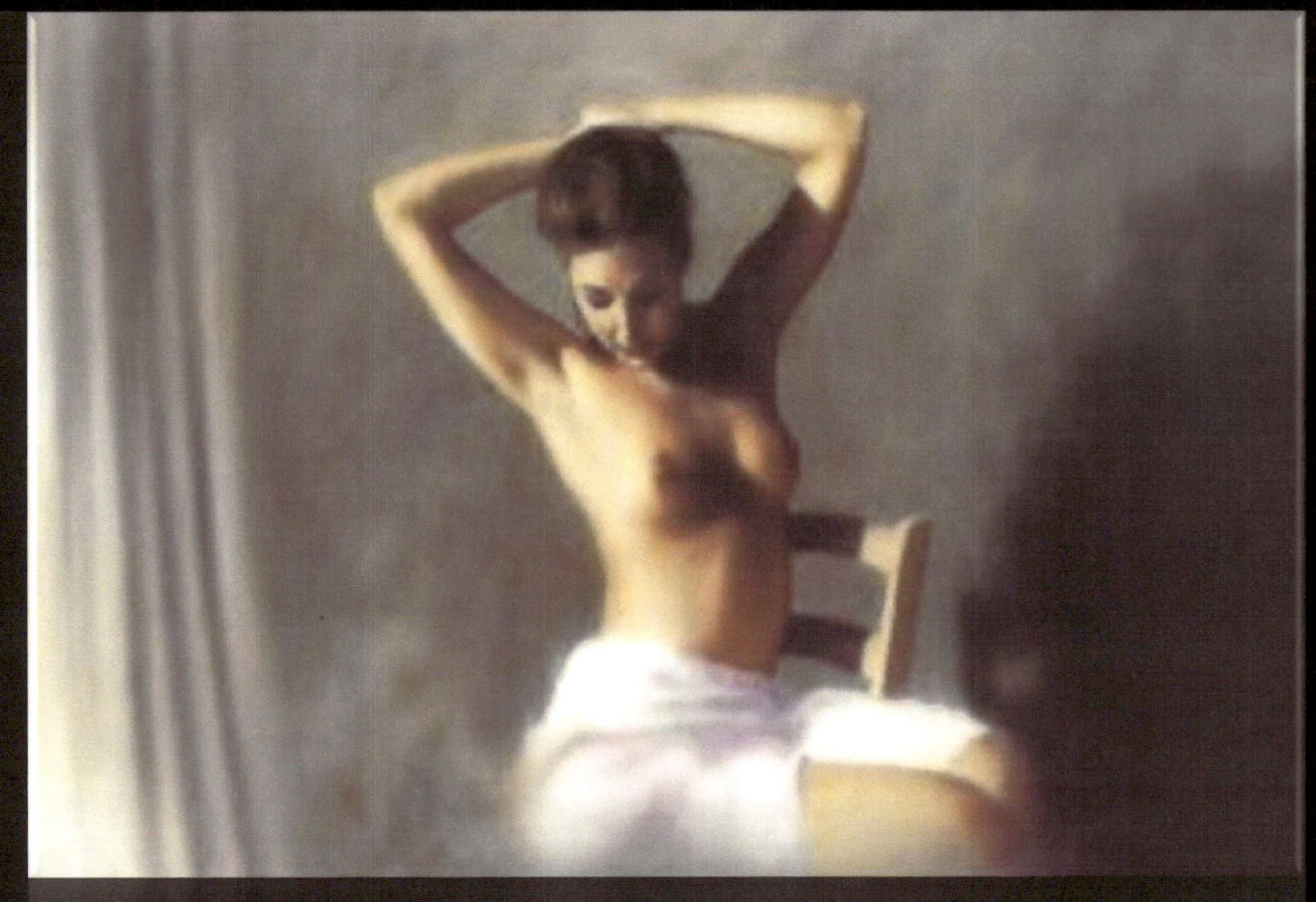

Pride By, Peter Worswick

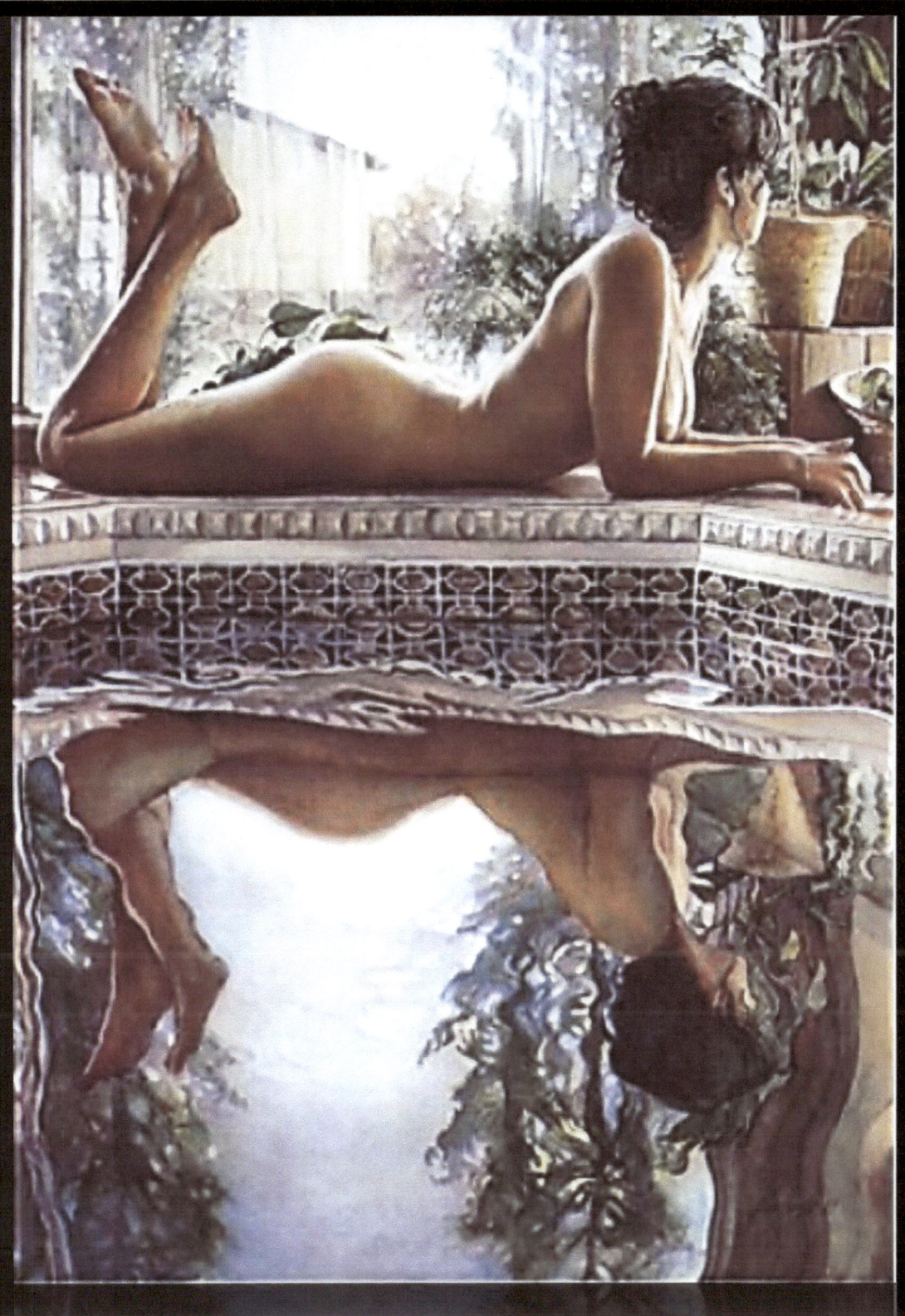

Reflecting Steve Hanks

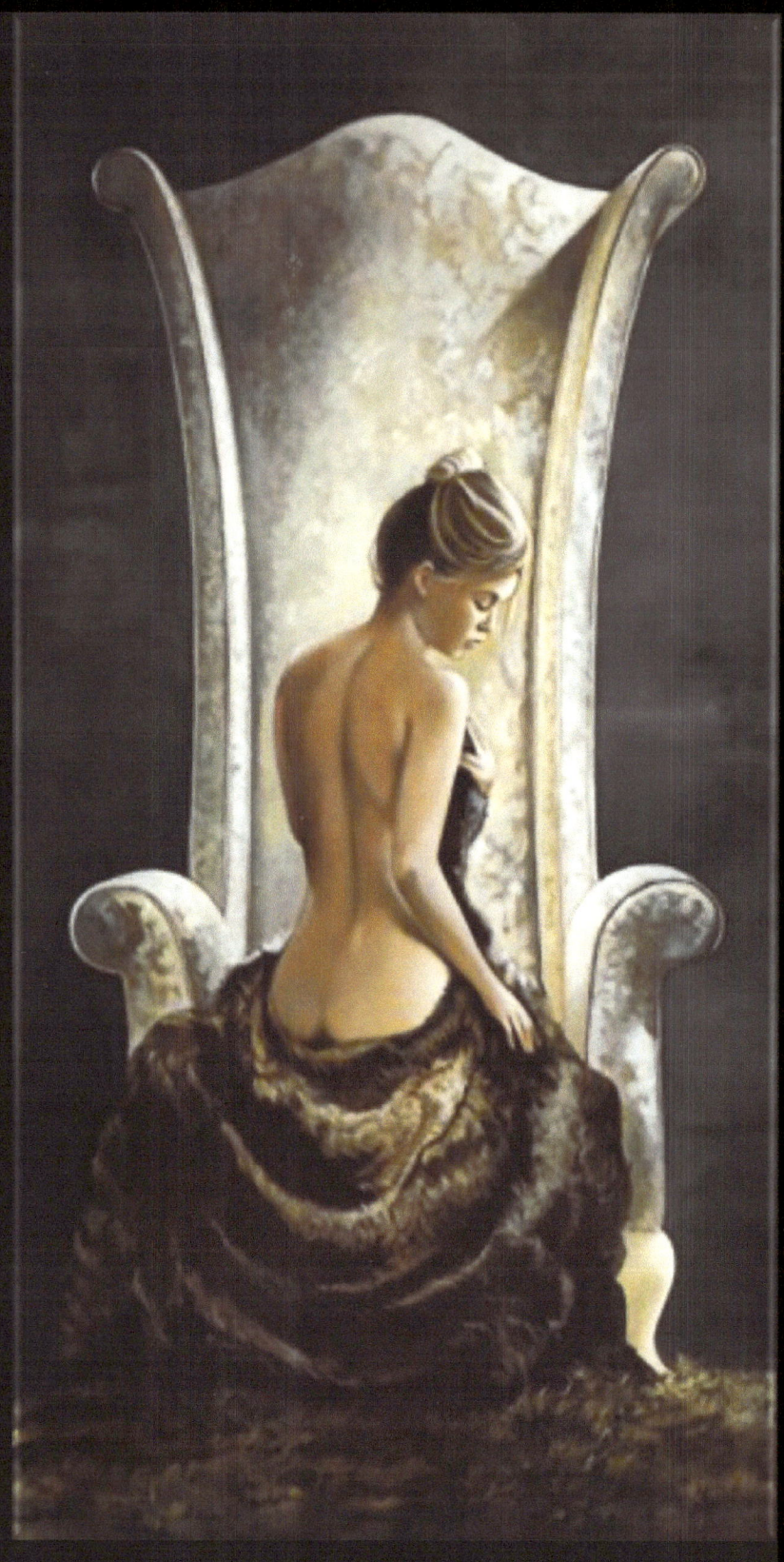

Lovely Lady Ron Di Scenza

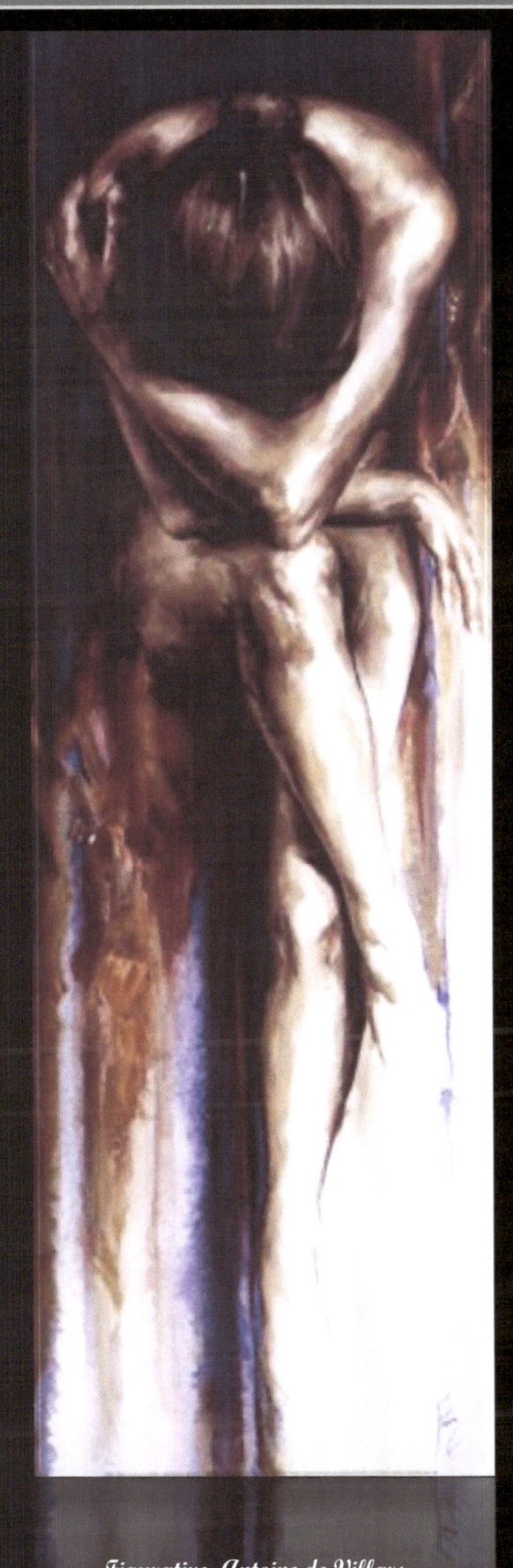

Figurative Antoine de Villars

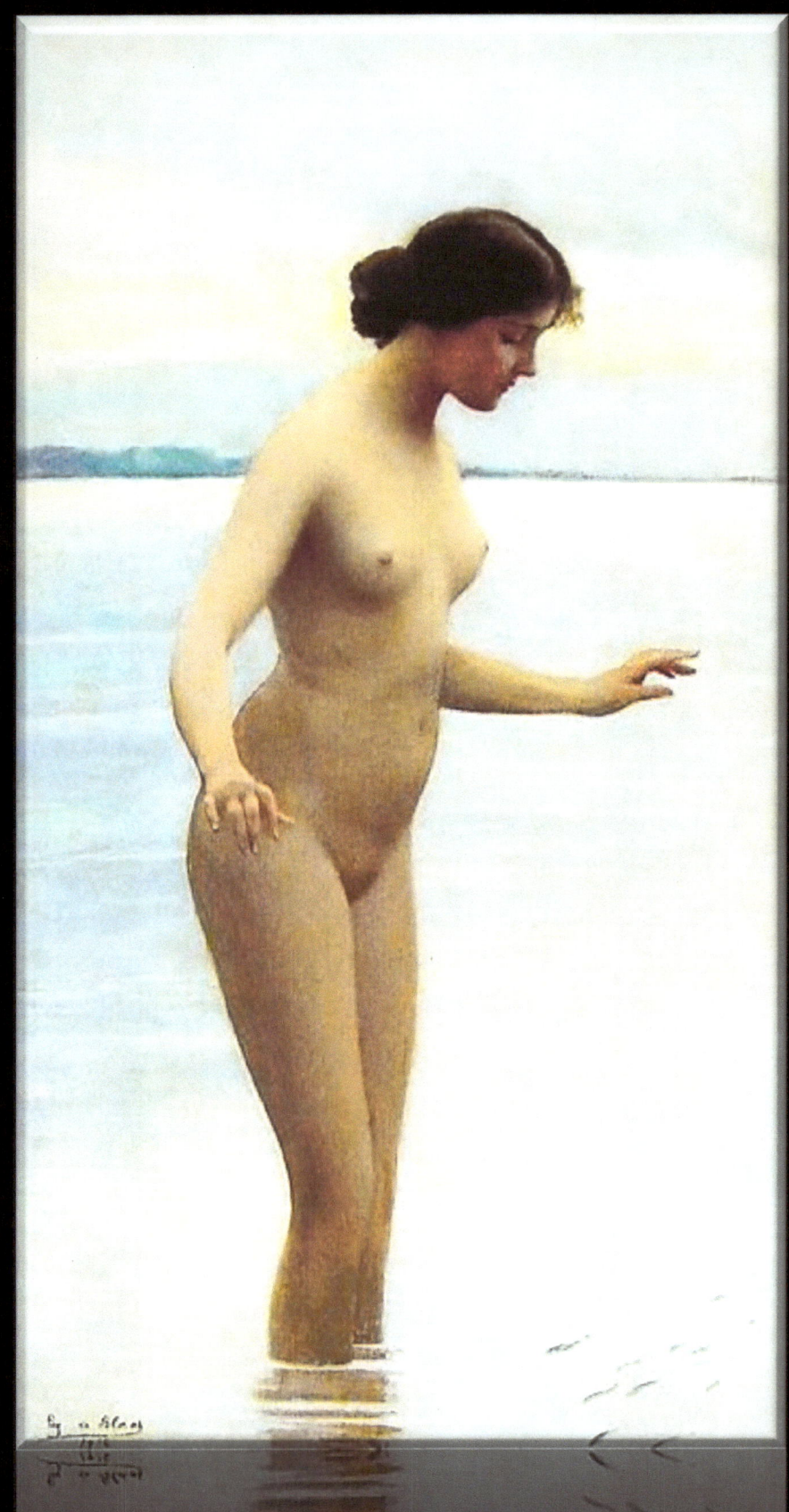

In the water (Dans l'Eau), oil on cradled panel painting by Italian painter Eugene de Blaas aka Eugen von Blaas (1843-1932)

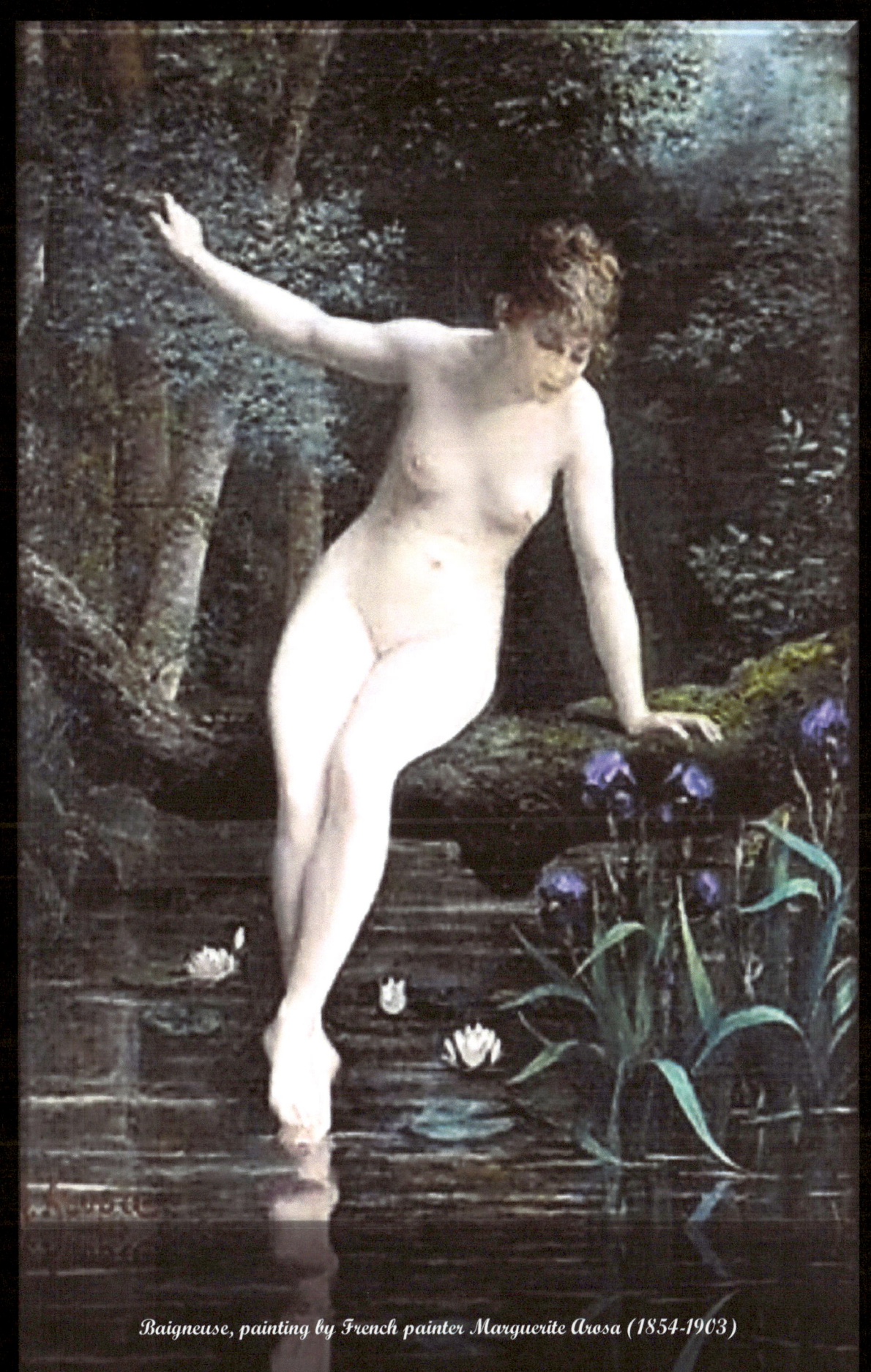

Baigneuse, painting by French painter Marguerite Arosa (1854-1903)

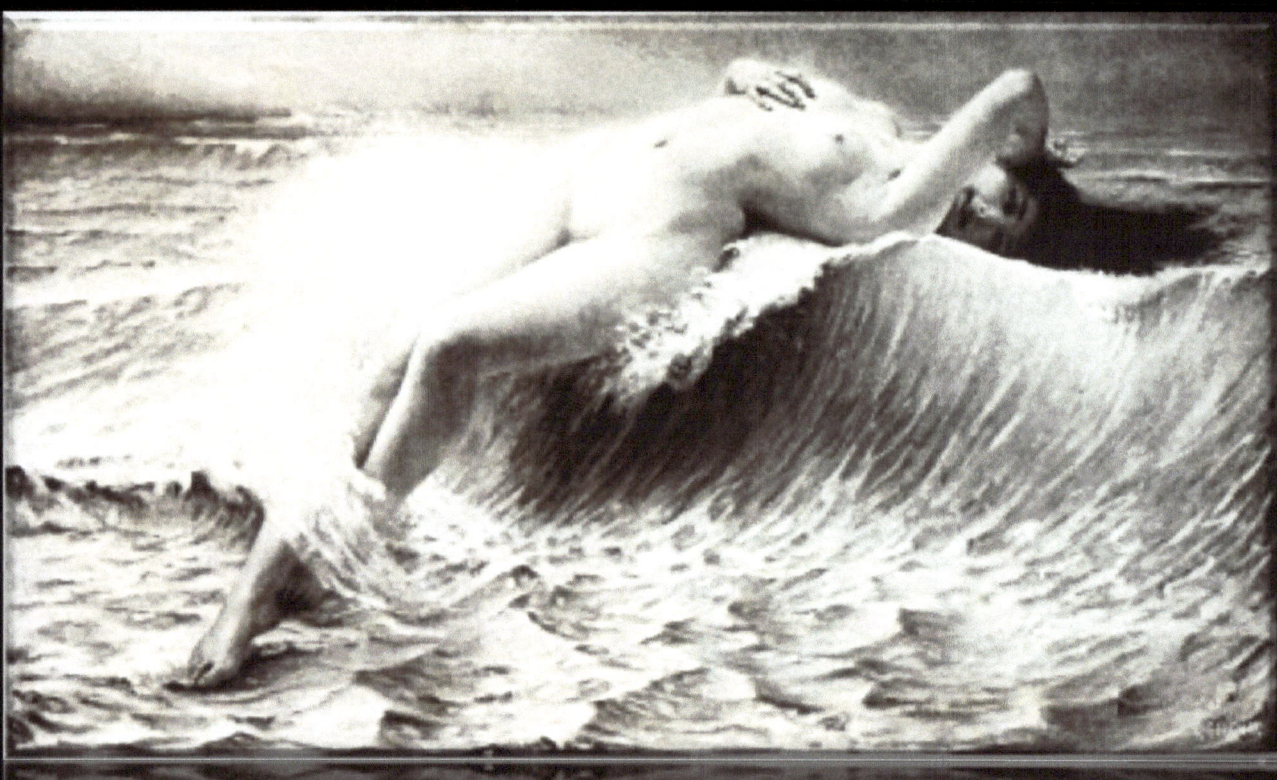

La Vague (1908) oil painting by French painter Guillaume Seignac (1870-1924).

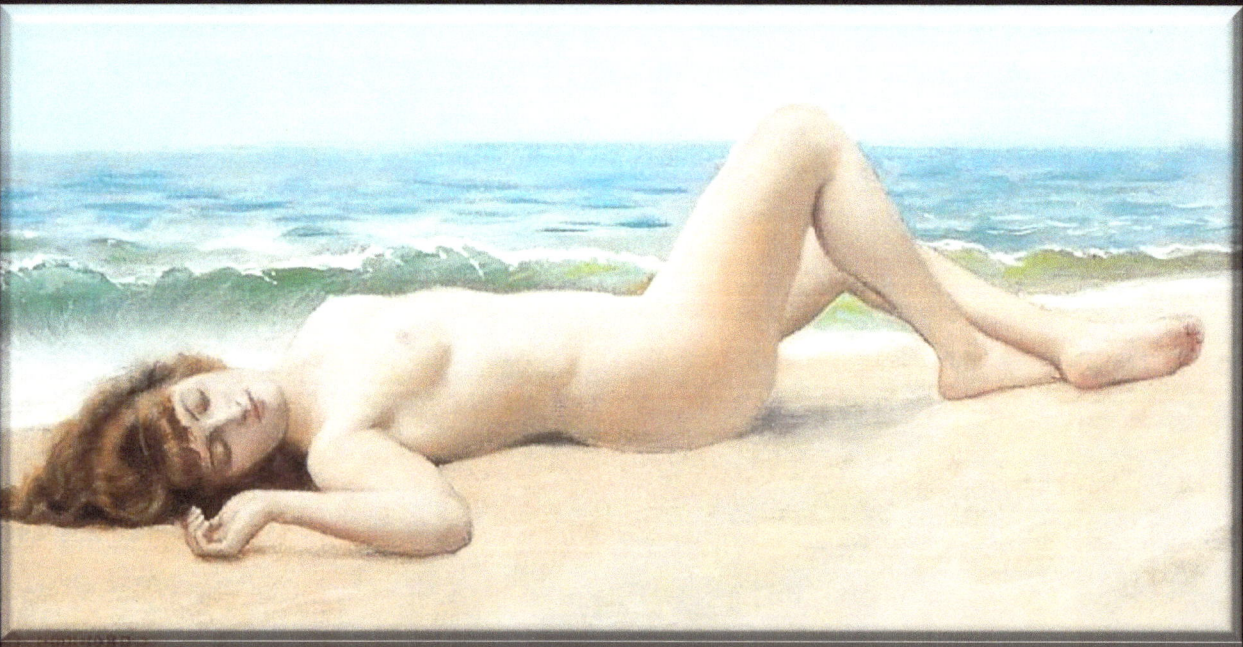

Nu Sur La Plage' (alternative name: Nude on the Beach), a 1922 oil on canvas painting by British painter John William Godward (1861-1922).

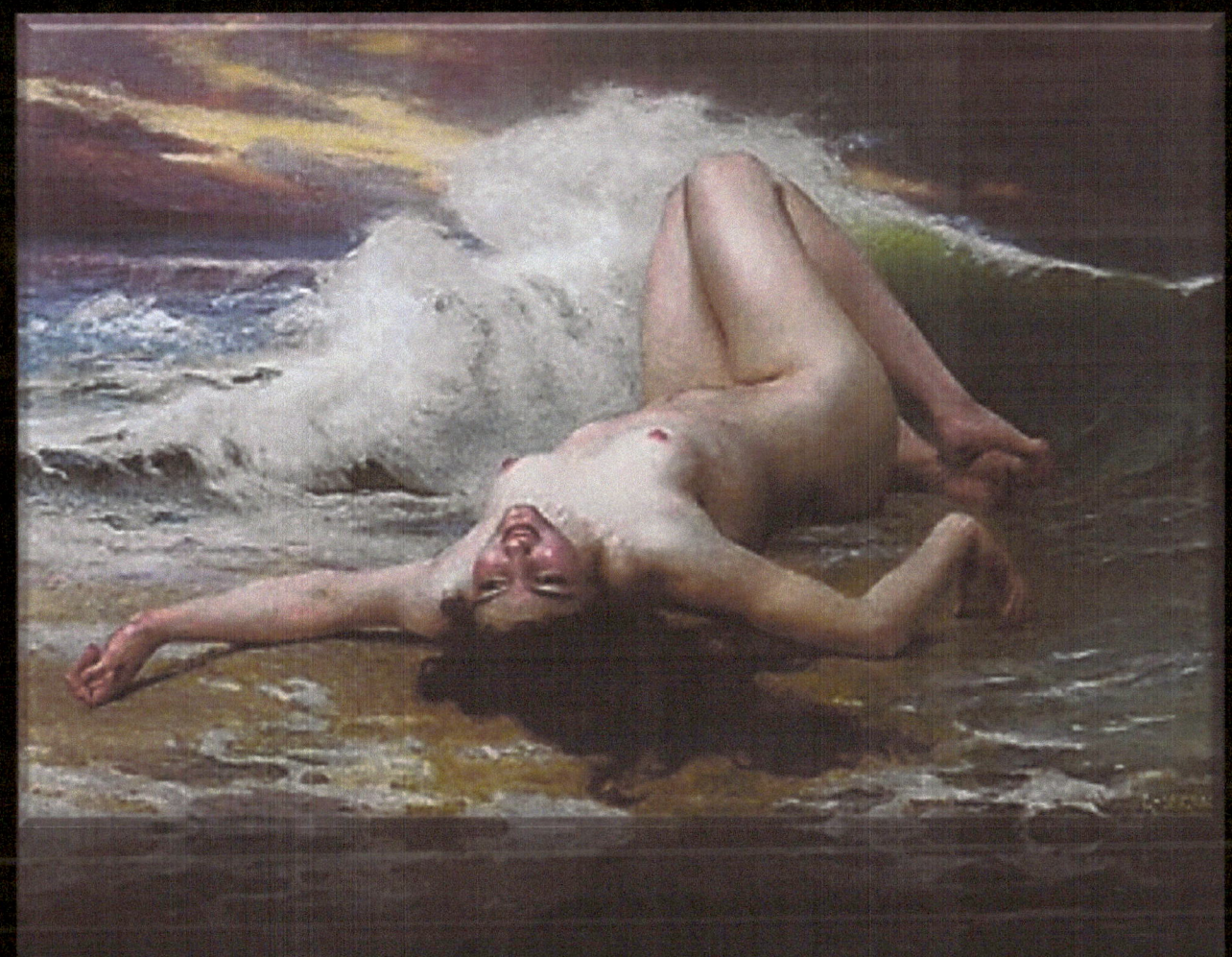

The Wave (alternate names: 'La Vague' or 'Fala') oil painting by French painter Guillaume Seignac (1870-1924).

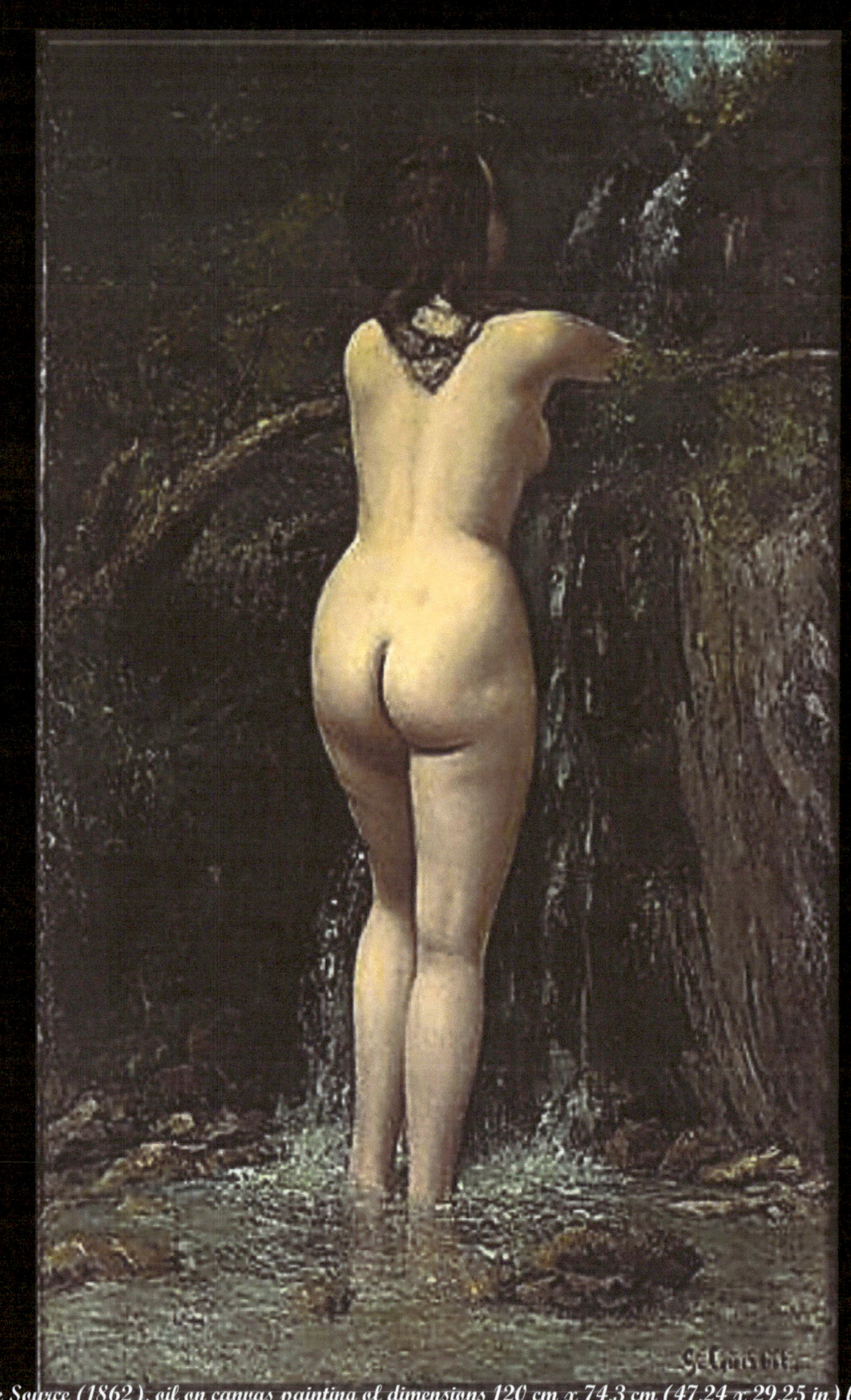

The Source (1862), oil on canvas painting of dimensions 120 cm x 74.3 cm (47.24 x 29.25 in) by French sculptor, painter and draughtsman Gustave Courbet (1819-1877)

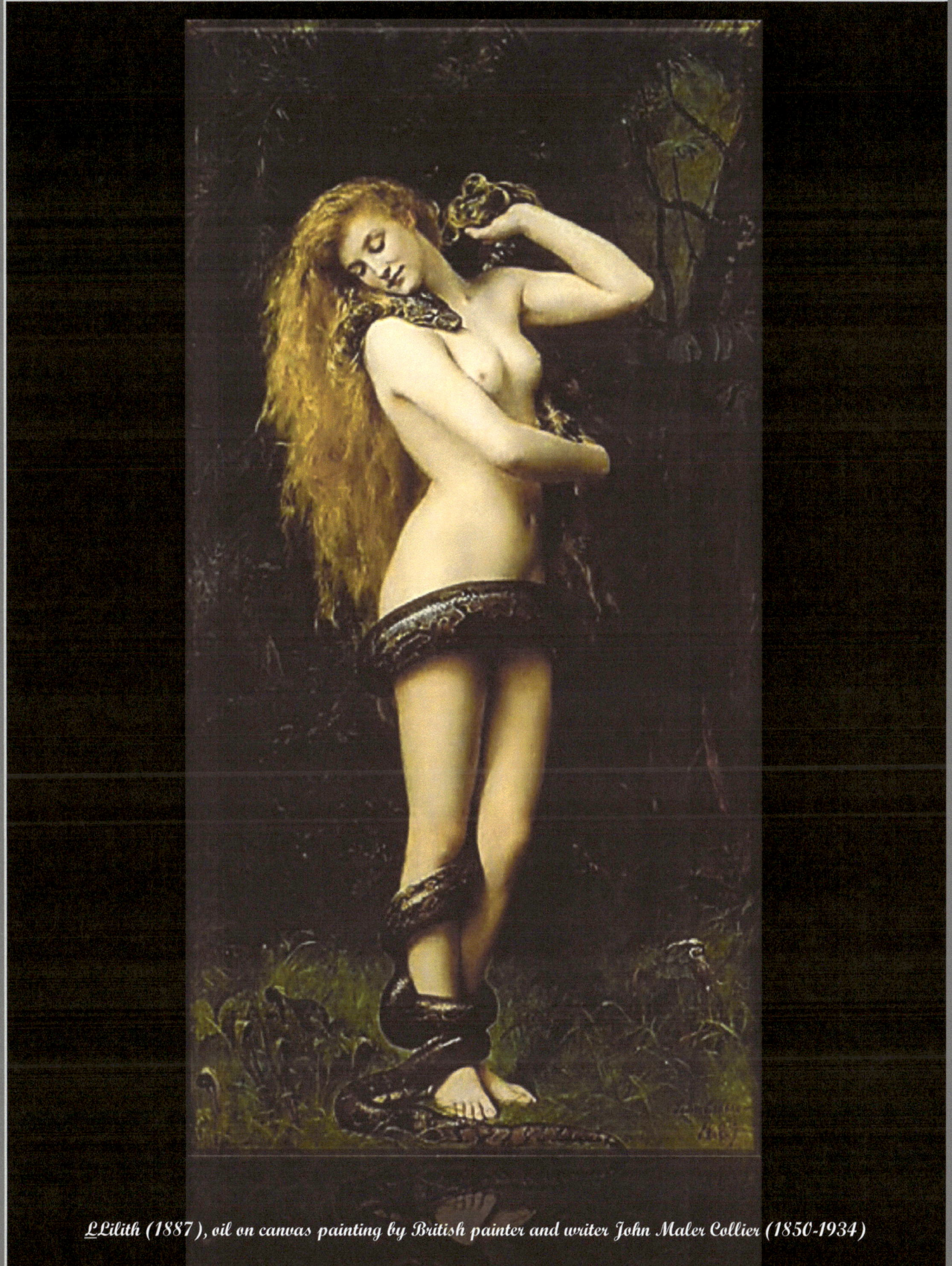

L.Lilith (1887), oil on canvas painting by British painter and writer John Maler Collier (1850-1934)

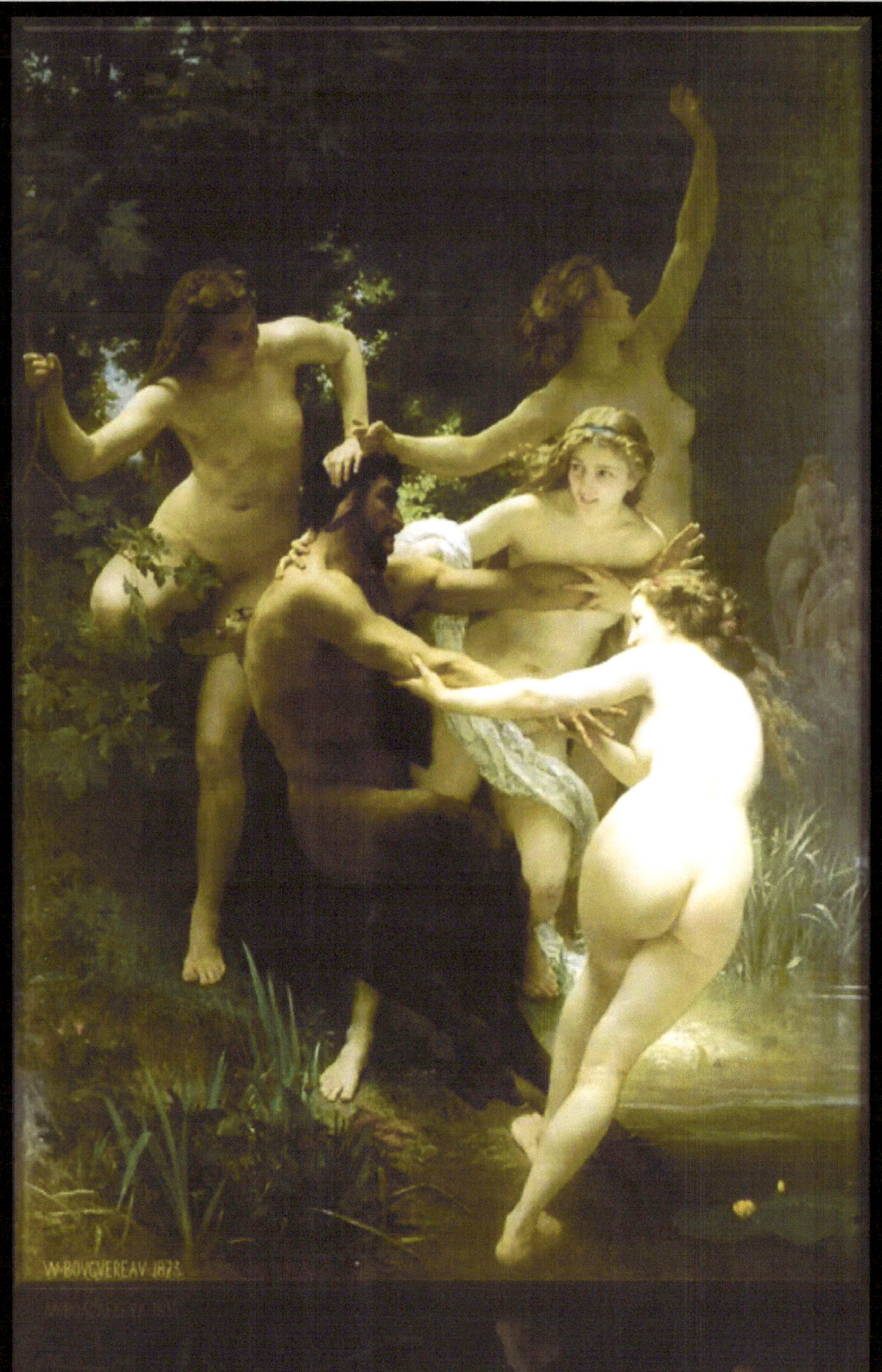

Nymphs and Satyr (Nymphes et Satires), oil on canvas, created by William-Adolphe Bouguereau in 1873

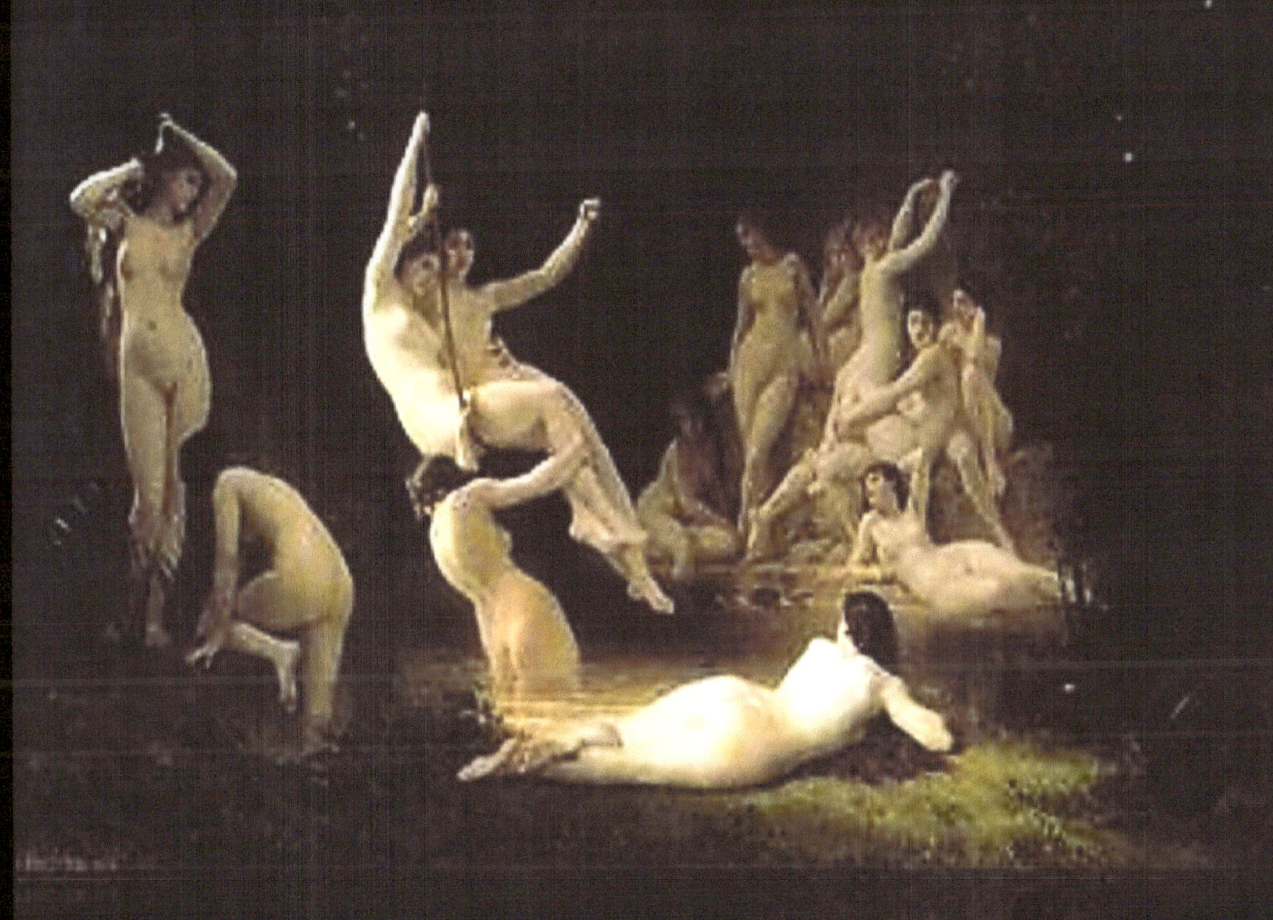

William-Adolphe Bouguereau (1825-1905) - The Nymphaeum (1878

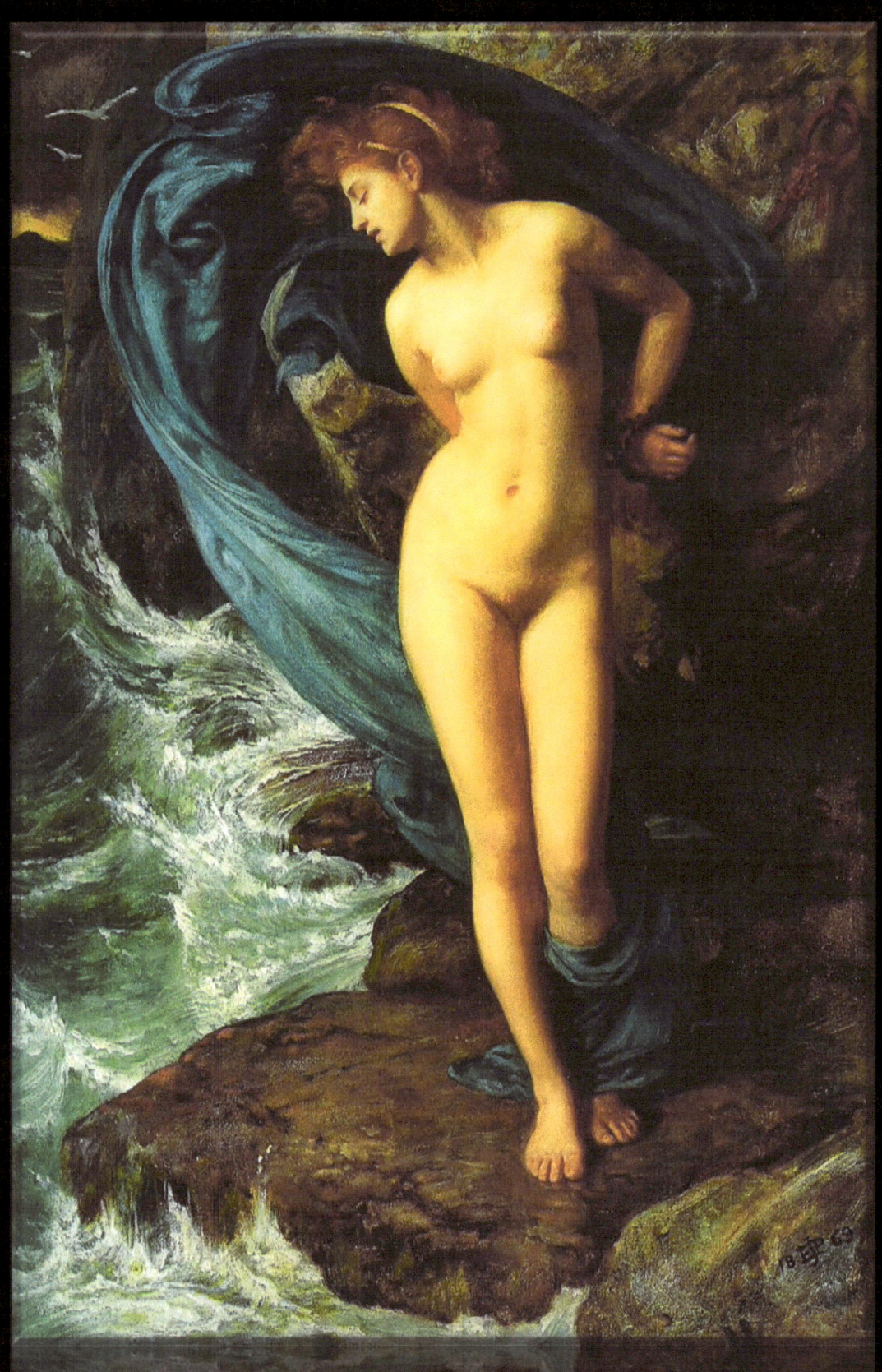

Paul Chabas*Andromeda' (1869), oil on canvas painting by British painter Sir Edward John Poynter (1836-1919)

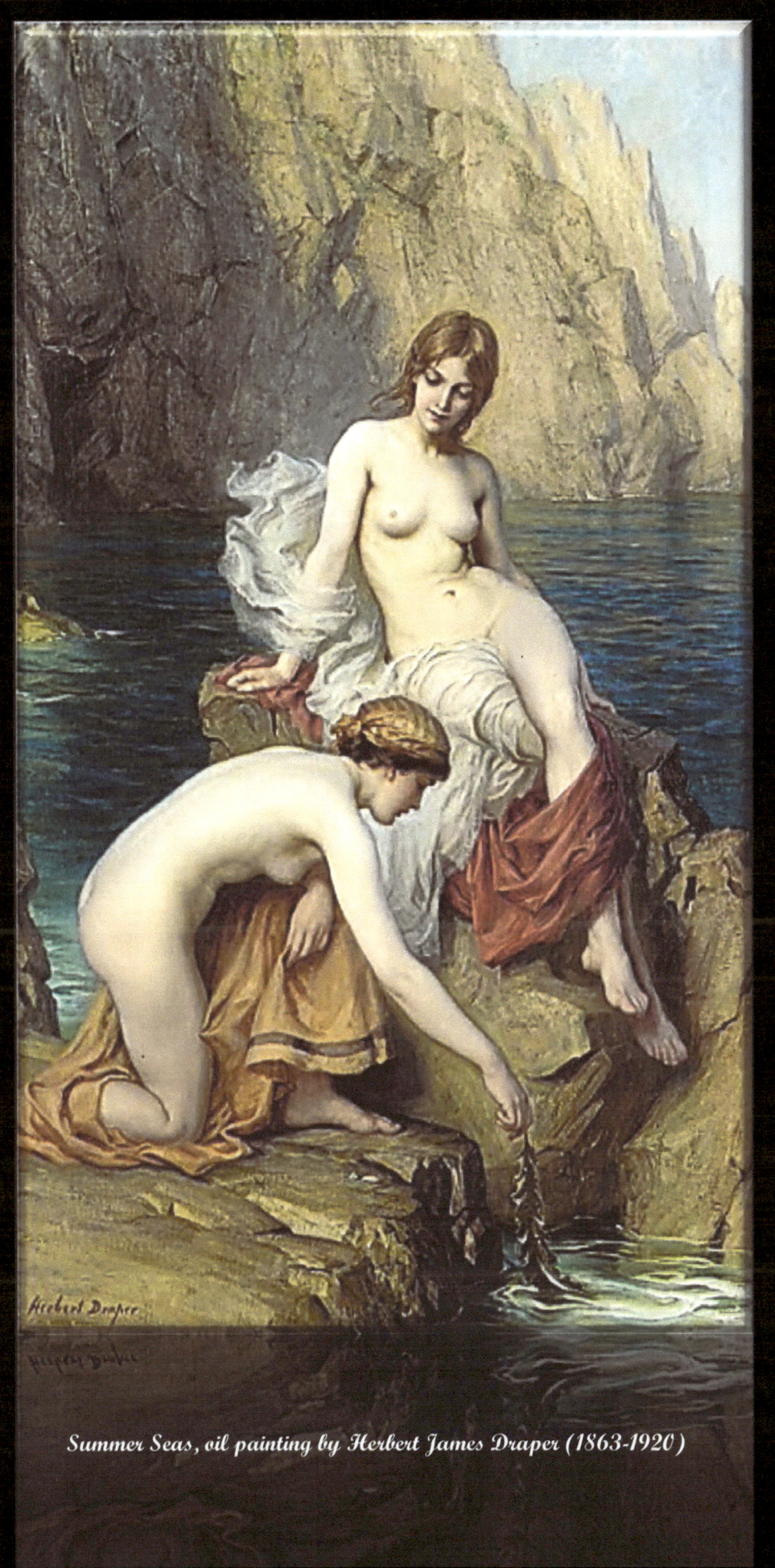

Summer Seas, oil painting by Herbert James Draper (1863-1920)

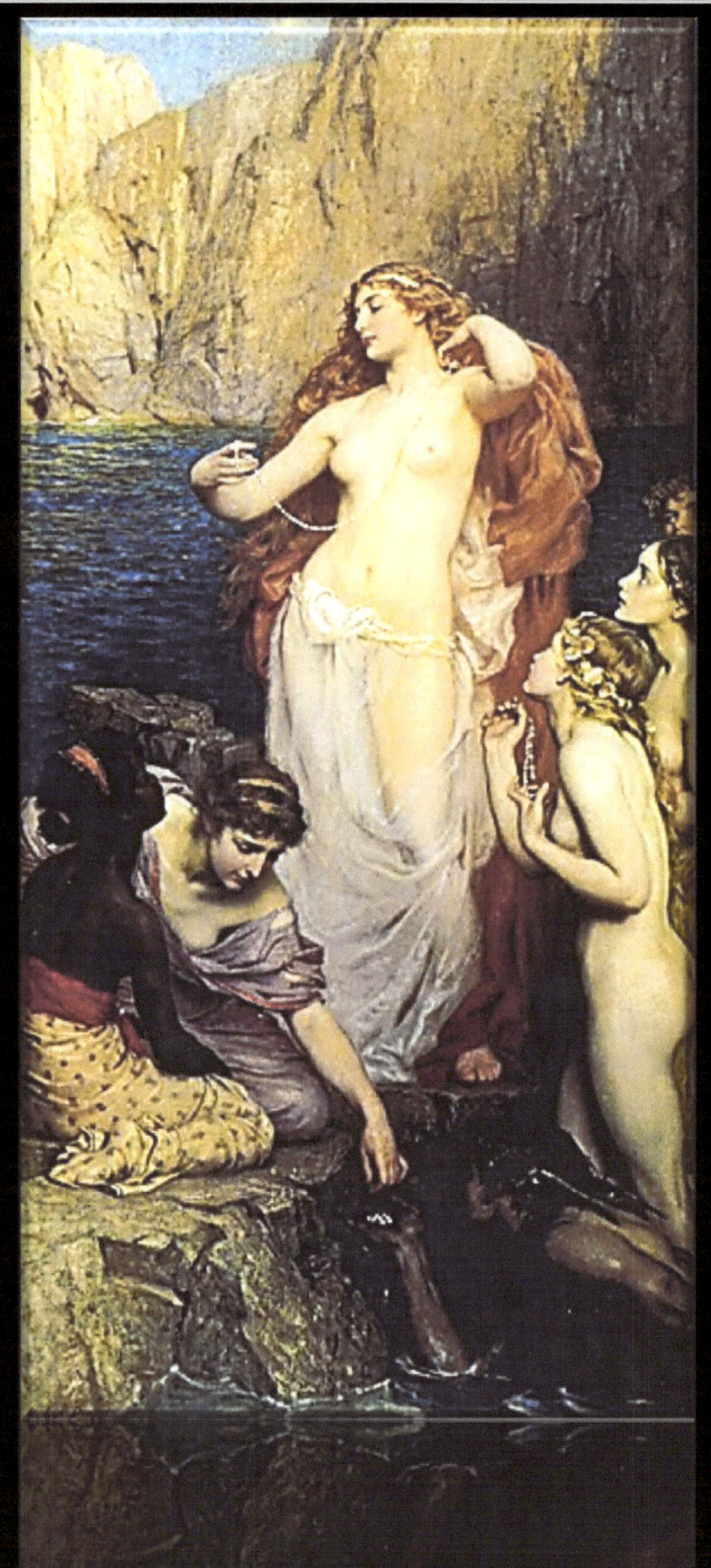

: *Pearls of Aphrodite, oil painting by Herbert James Draper (1863-1920)*

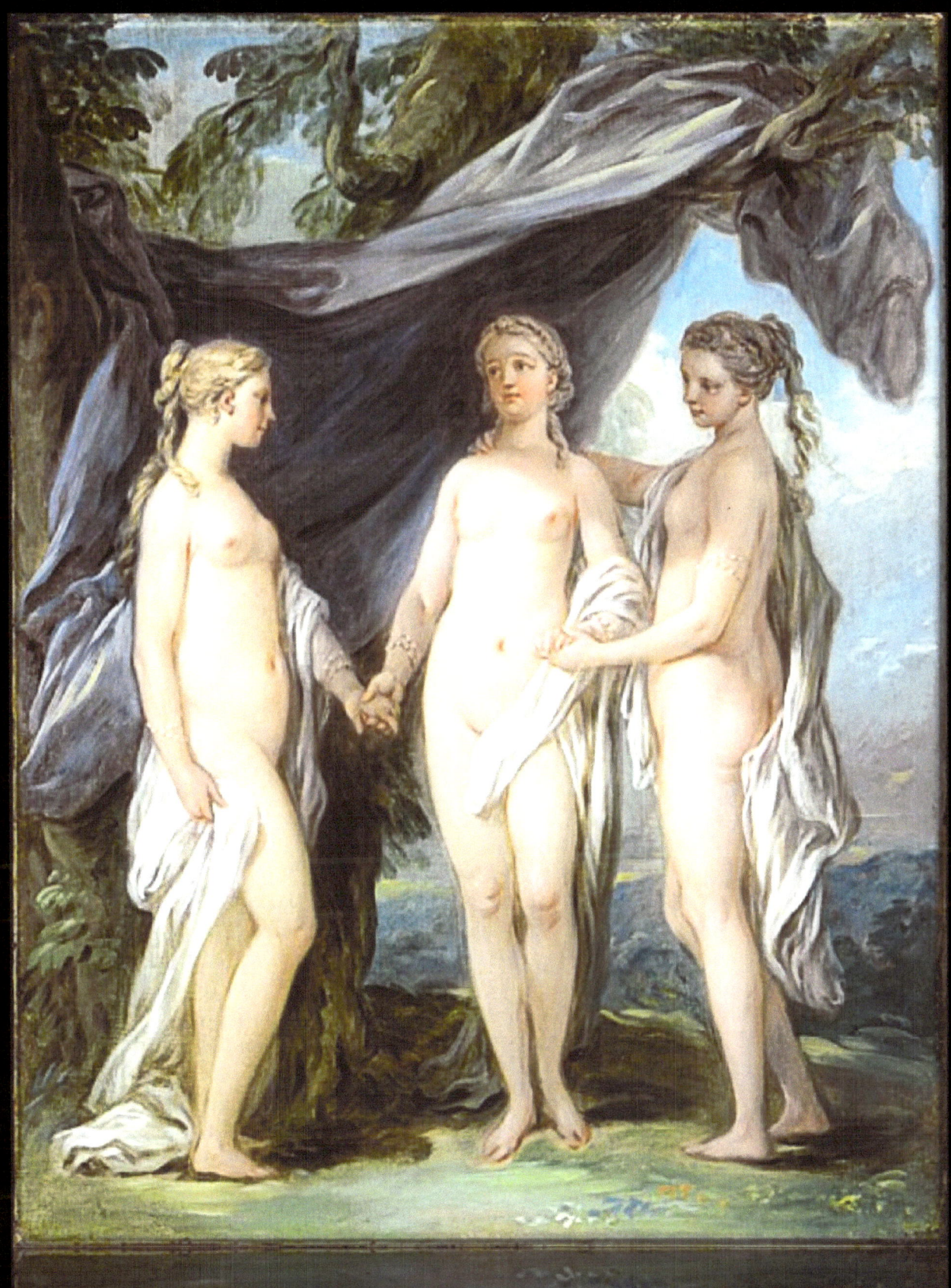

The Three Graces (Les-Trois-Grâces), created in 1763 by Charles André van Loo (1705-1765

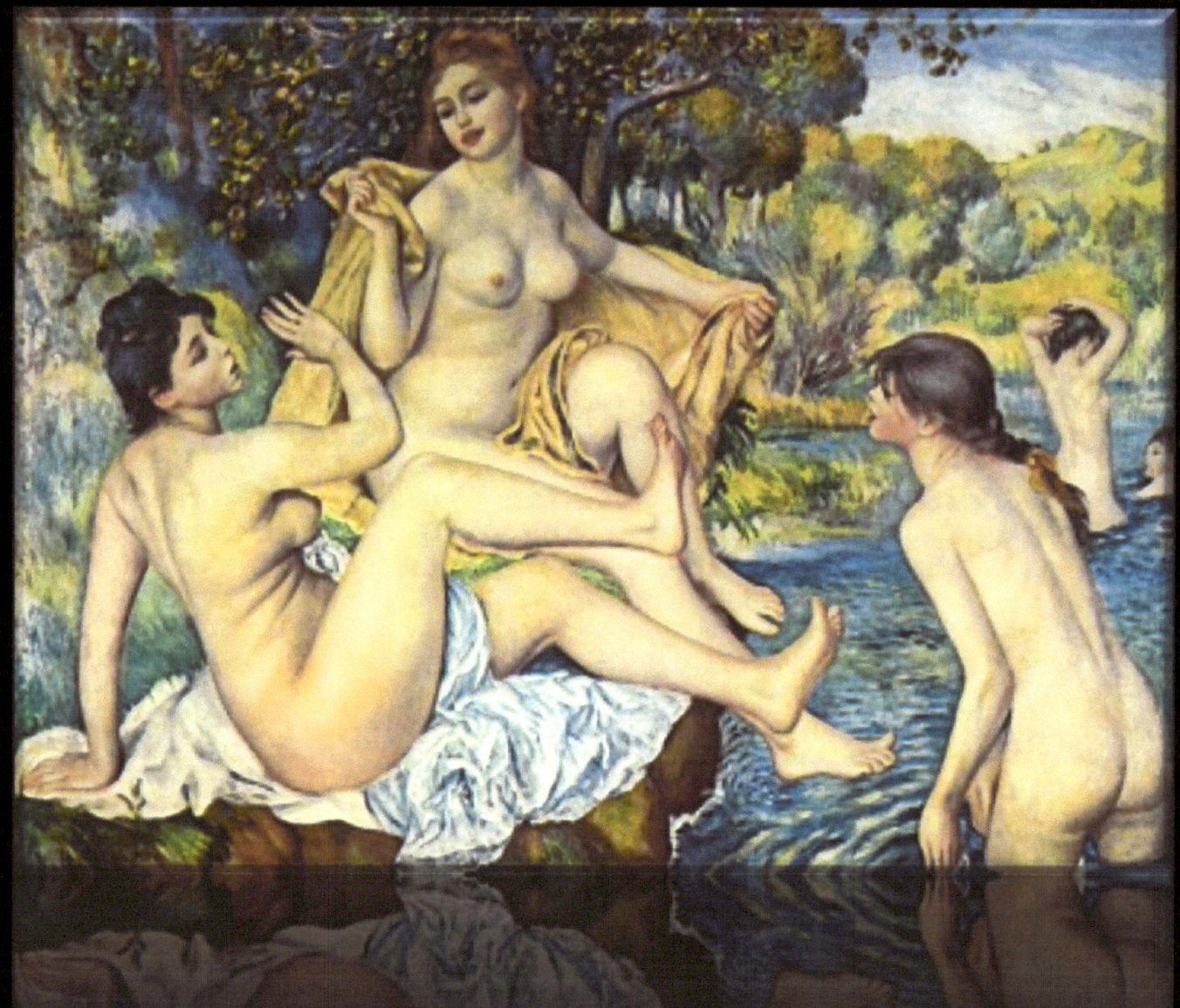

The Large Bathers (1887), oil on canvas painting by French painter Pierre-Auguste Renoir (1841-1919),

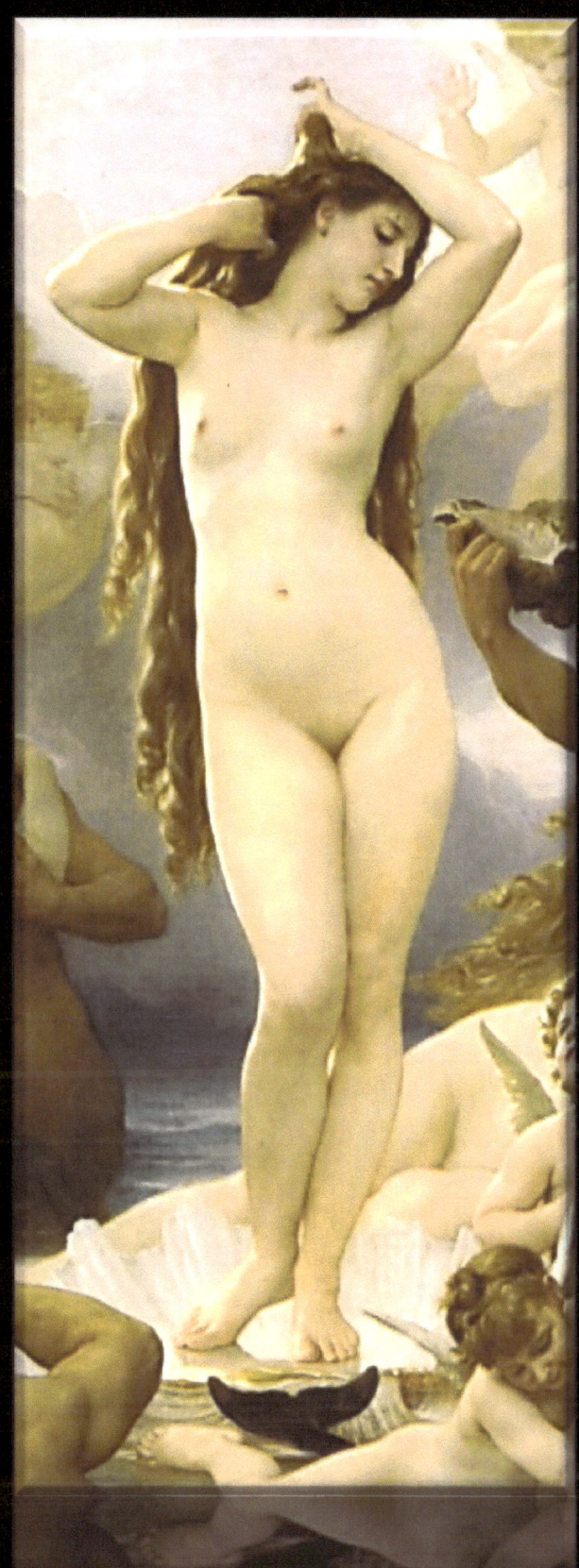

The Birth of Venus by Bouguereau (1879).

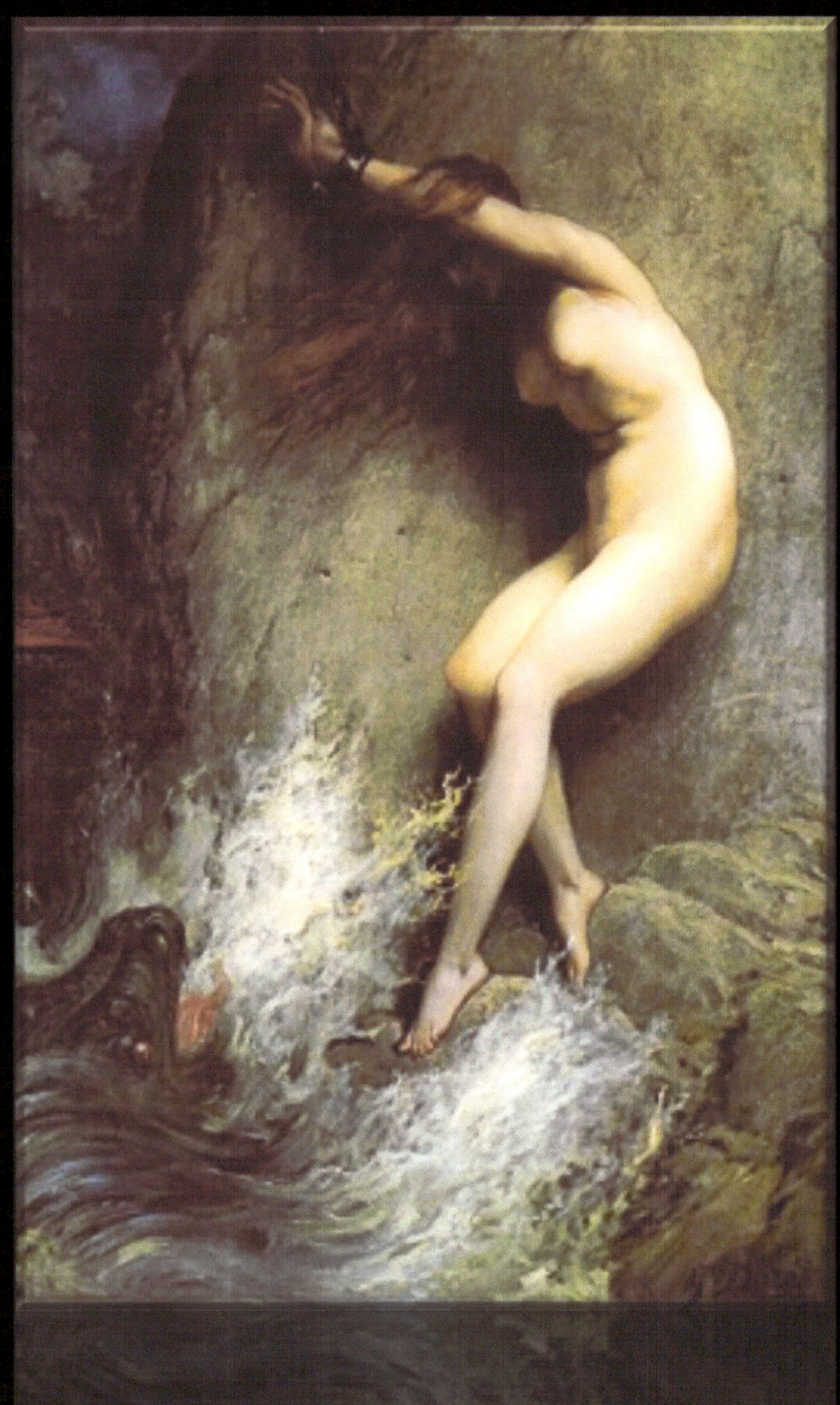

'Andromeda chained to a rock' (1869) by French artist, engraver, illustrator and sculptor Paul Gustave Doré (1832-1883

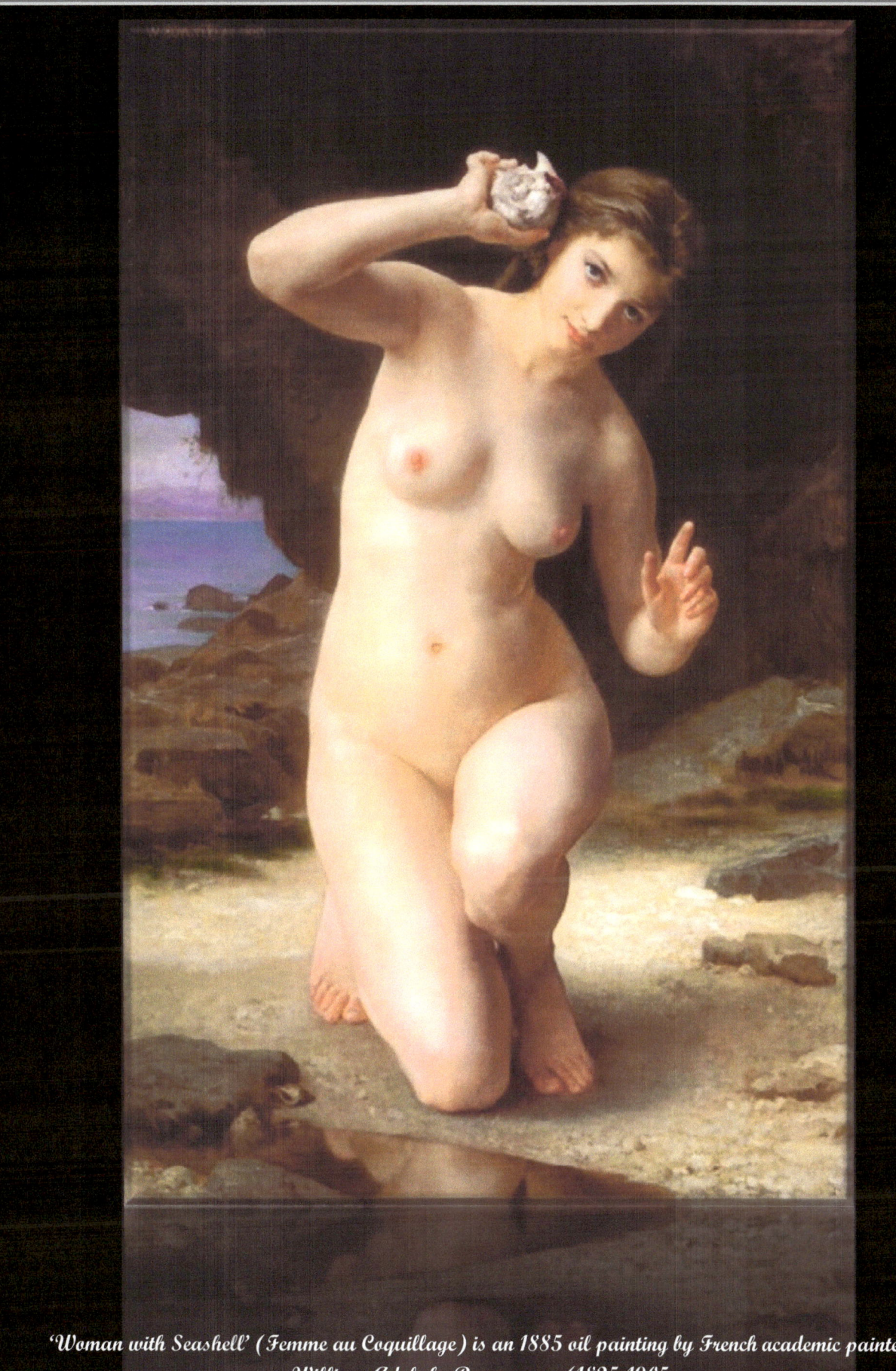

'Woman with Seashell' (Femme au Coquillage) is an 1885 oil painting by French academic painter William-Adolphe Bouguereau (1825-1905

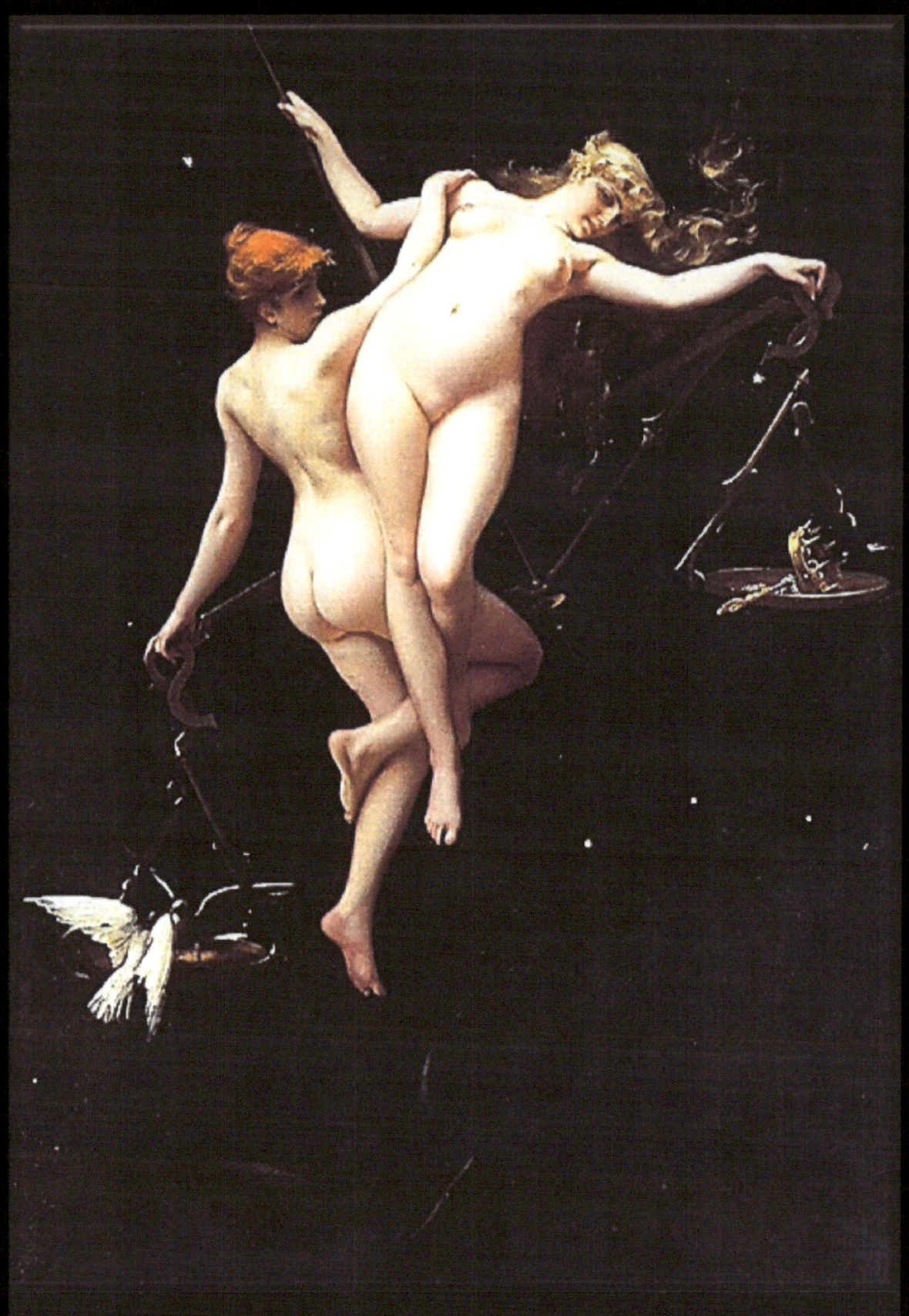

Painted in 1886 by Emmanuel de DieudonnéThe Balance of the Zodiac (La Balance du Zodiaque), oil on panel painting by Spanish painter Luis Ricardo Falero (1851-1896)

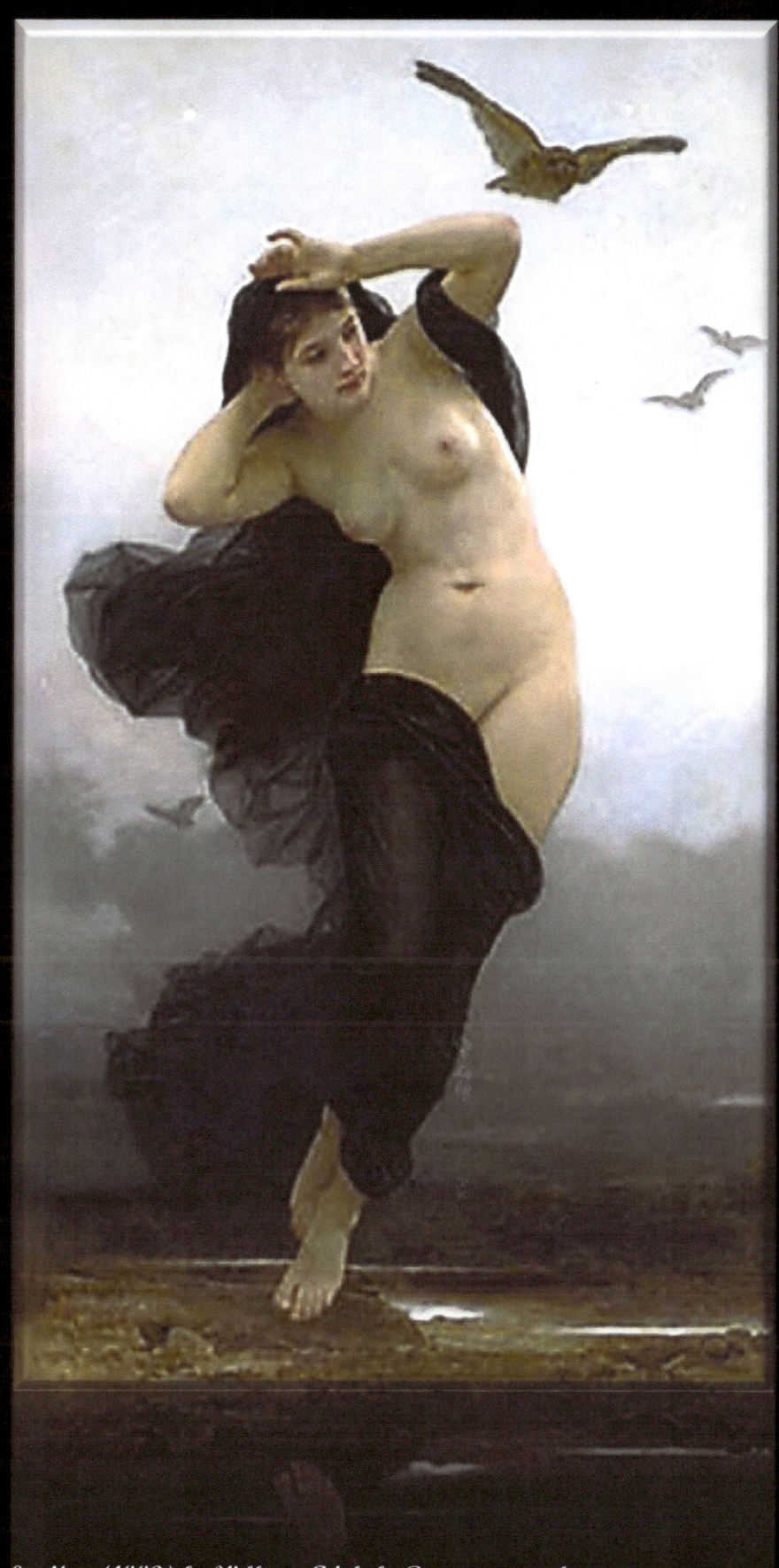

La Nuit (1883) by William-Adolphe Bouguereau, oil on canvas painting.

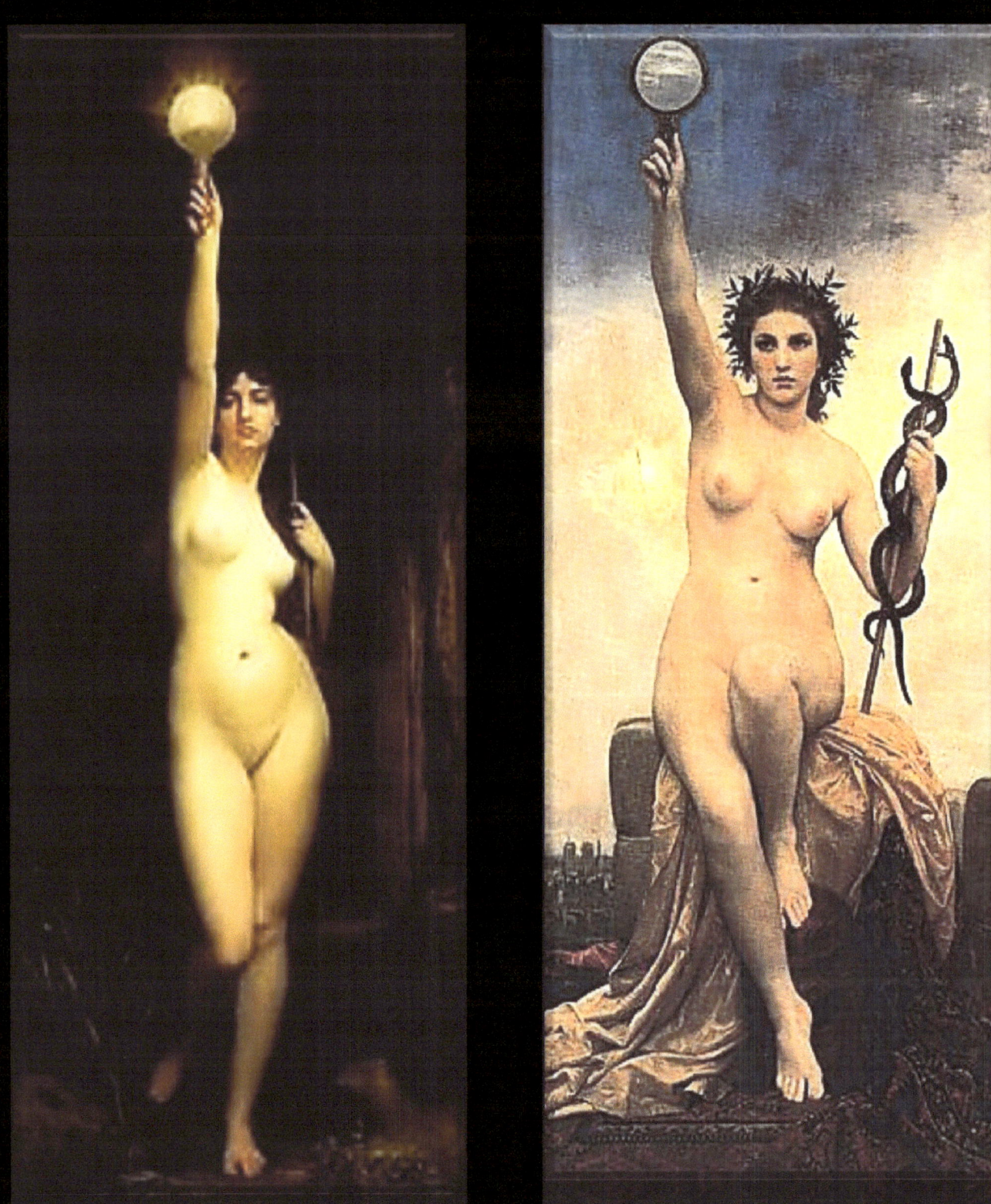

Shown to the right is <u>William-Adolphe Bouguereau</u> (1825–1905) Description
English: Integrity1876

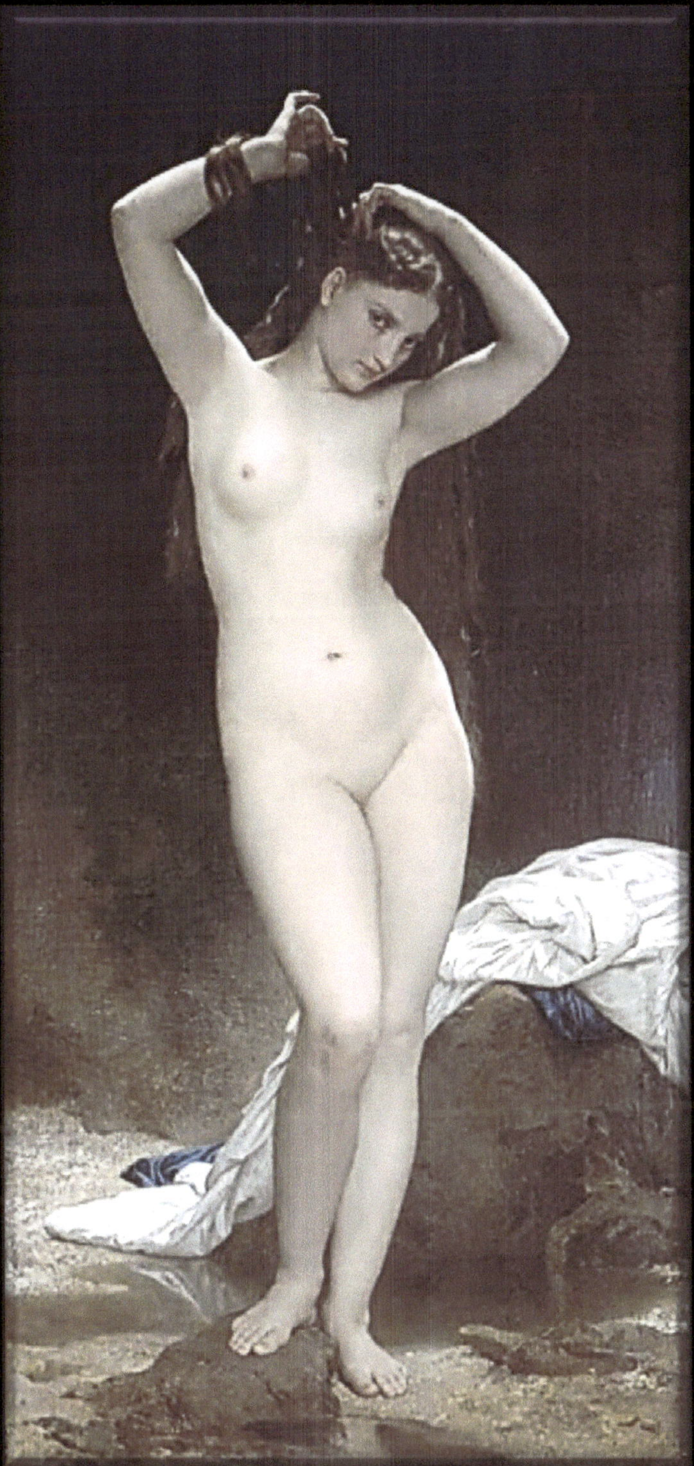

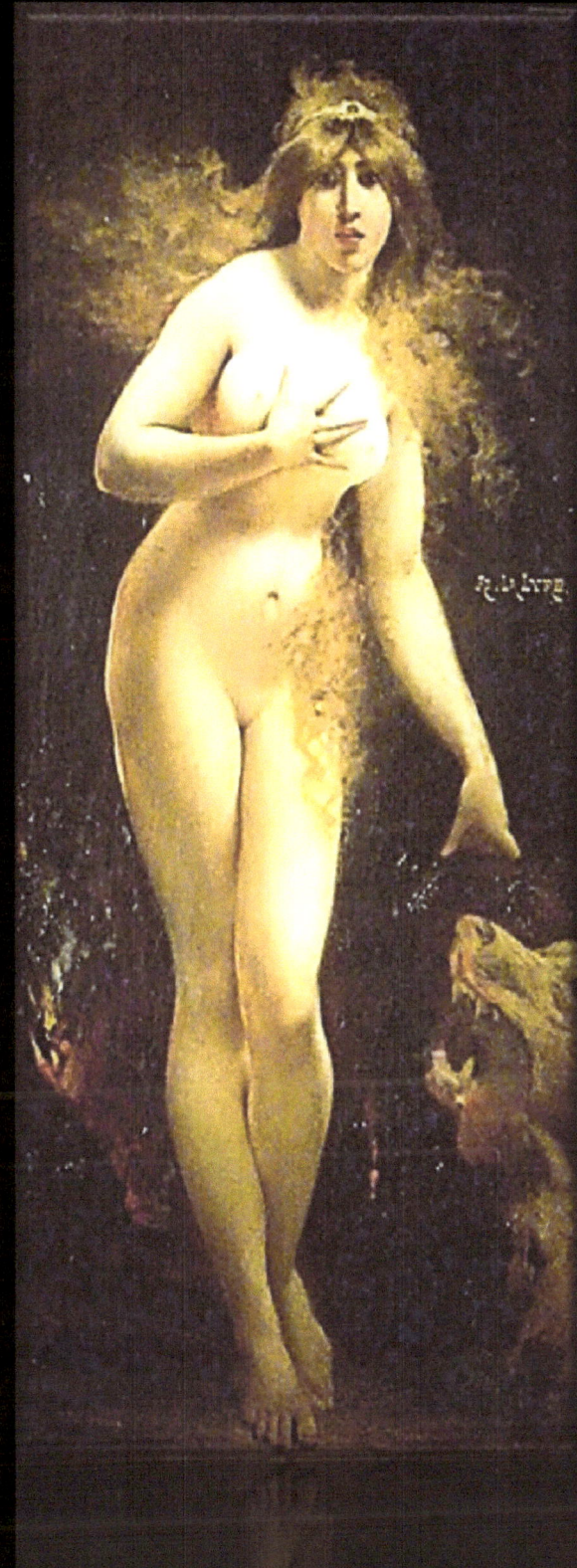

artist Adolphe La Lyre (1848-1933), Bather (1870) by French academic painter William-Adolphe Bouguereau

Psyché aux enfers (1904), oil on canvas painting by French

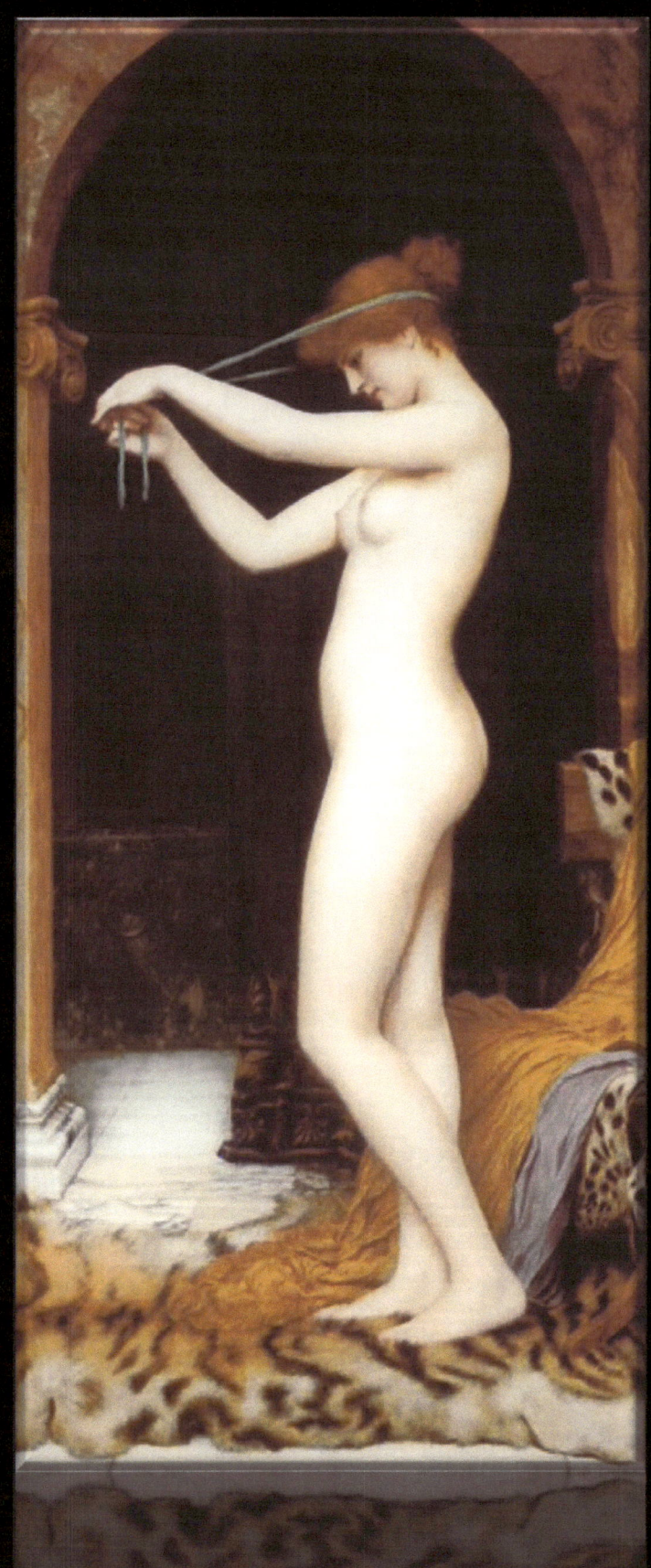

Venus Binding Her Hair (Vénus nouant ses cheveux), oil on canvas painting (1897) by the British painter

John William Godward (1861-1922)

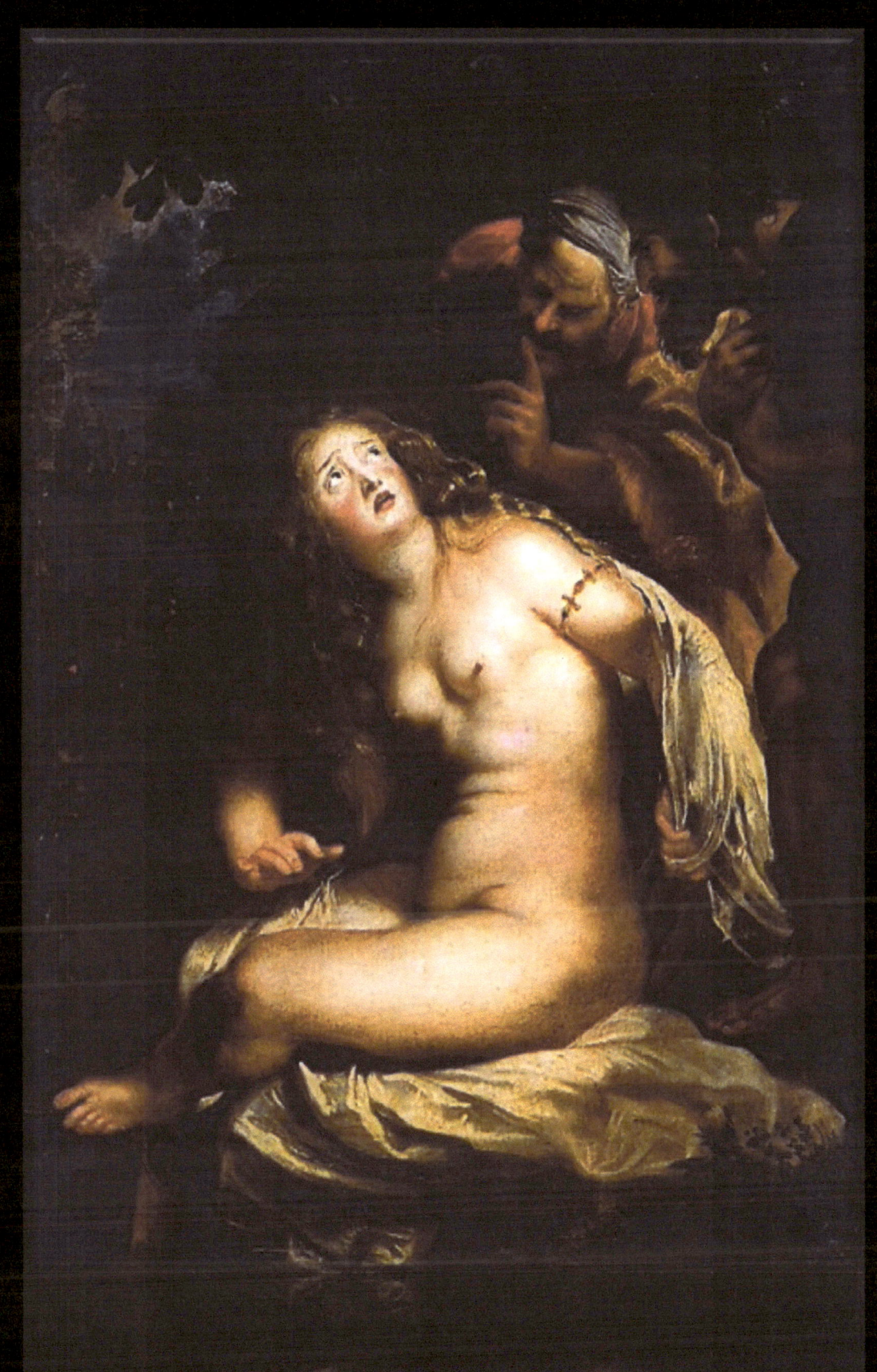

Susanna and the Elders (1607-08), oil on canvas painting by seventeenth-century Flemish Baroque painter Sir Peter Paul Rubens (1577-1640)

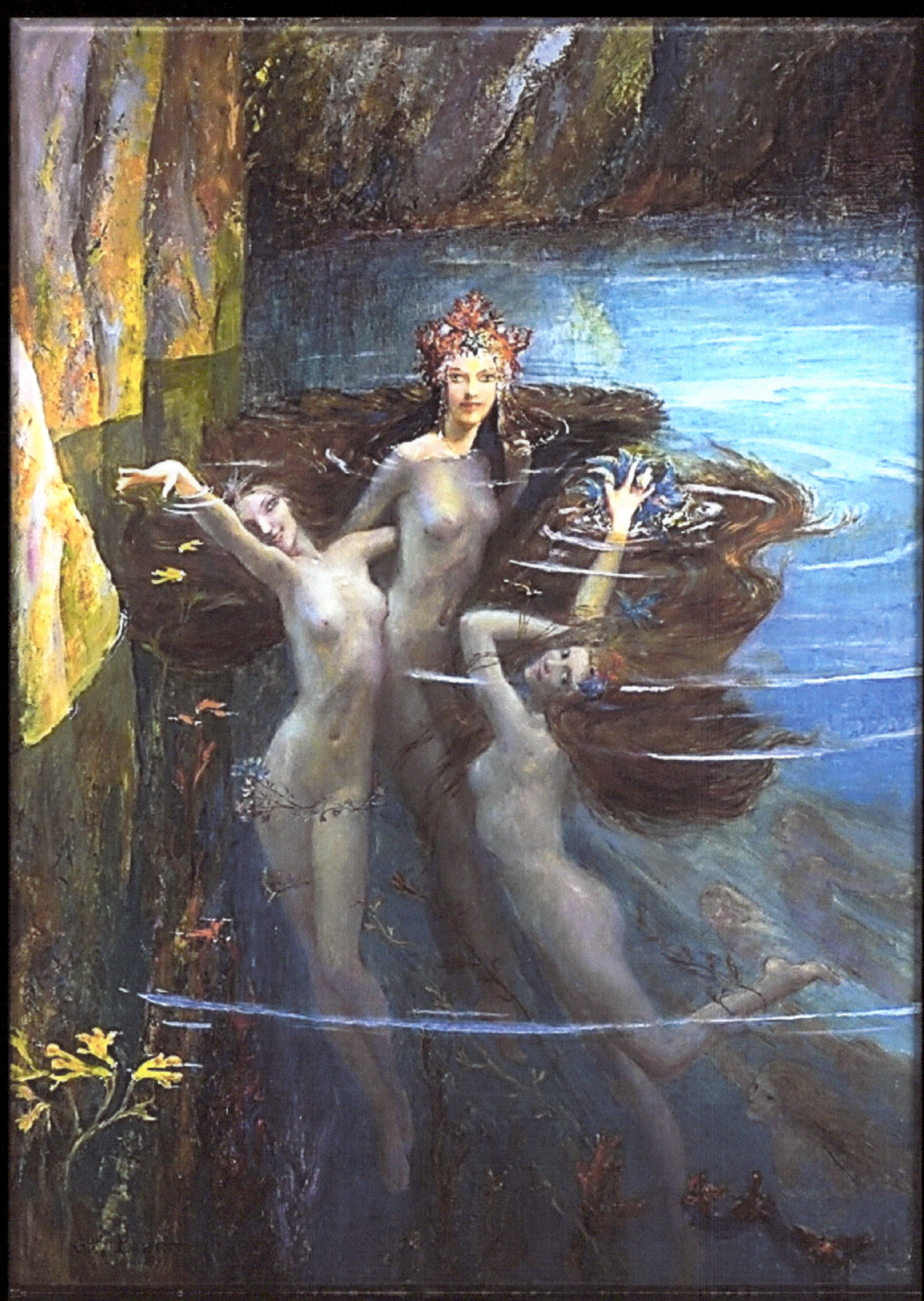

The Nereides (1902), oil on canvas painting by French painter and illustrator Gaston Bussiere (1862-1929),

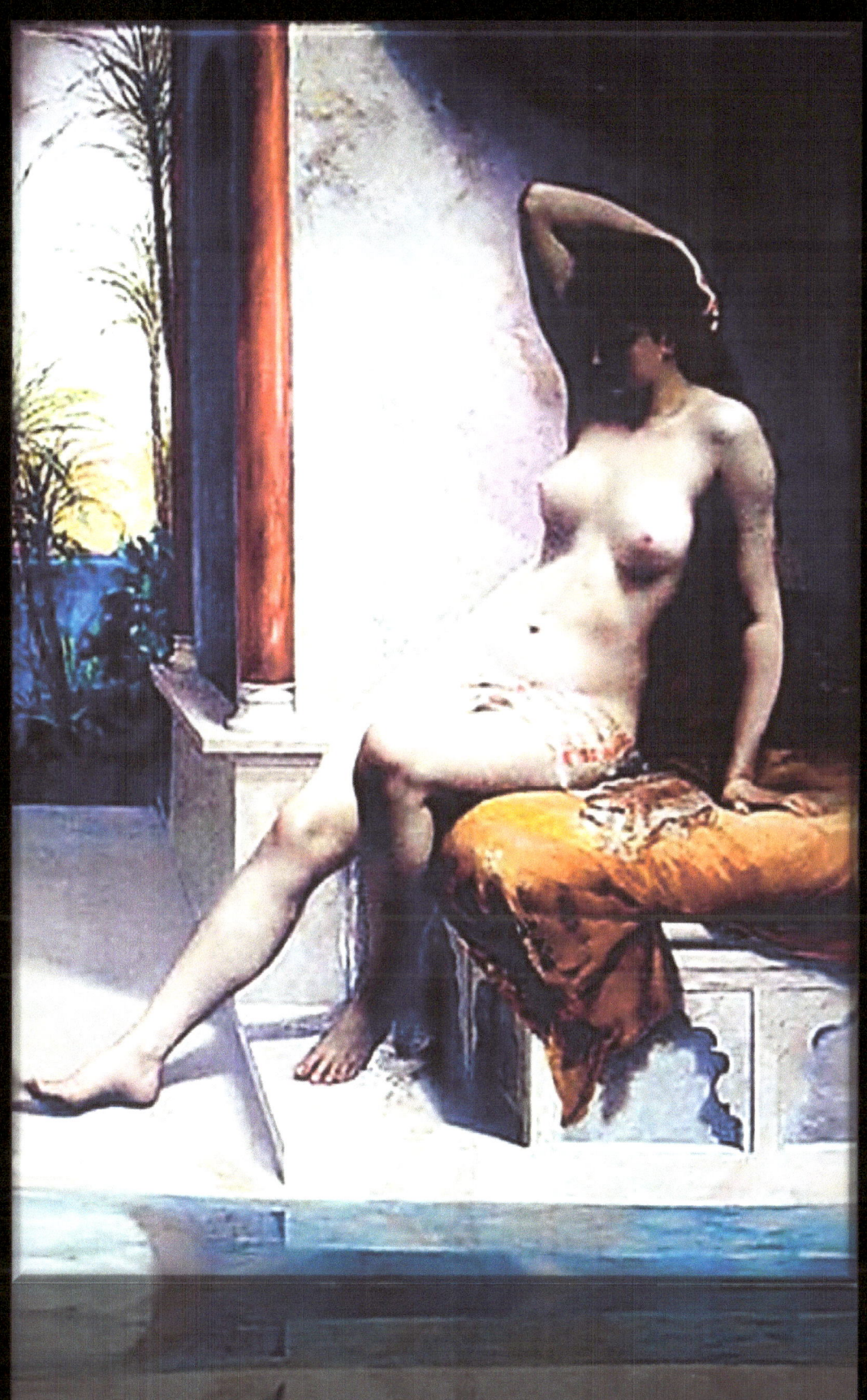

A bela no banho (Beauty in the bath) oil on canvas, painted in 1886 by Emmanuel de Dieudonné, dimensions

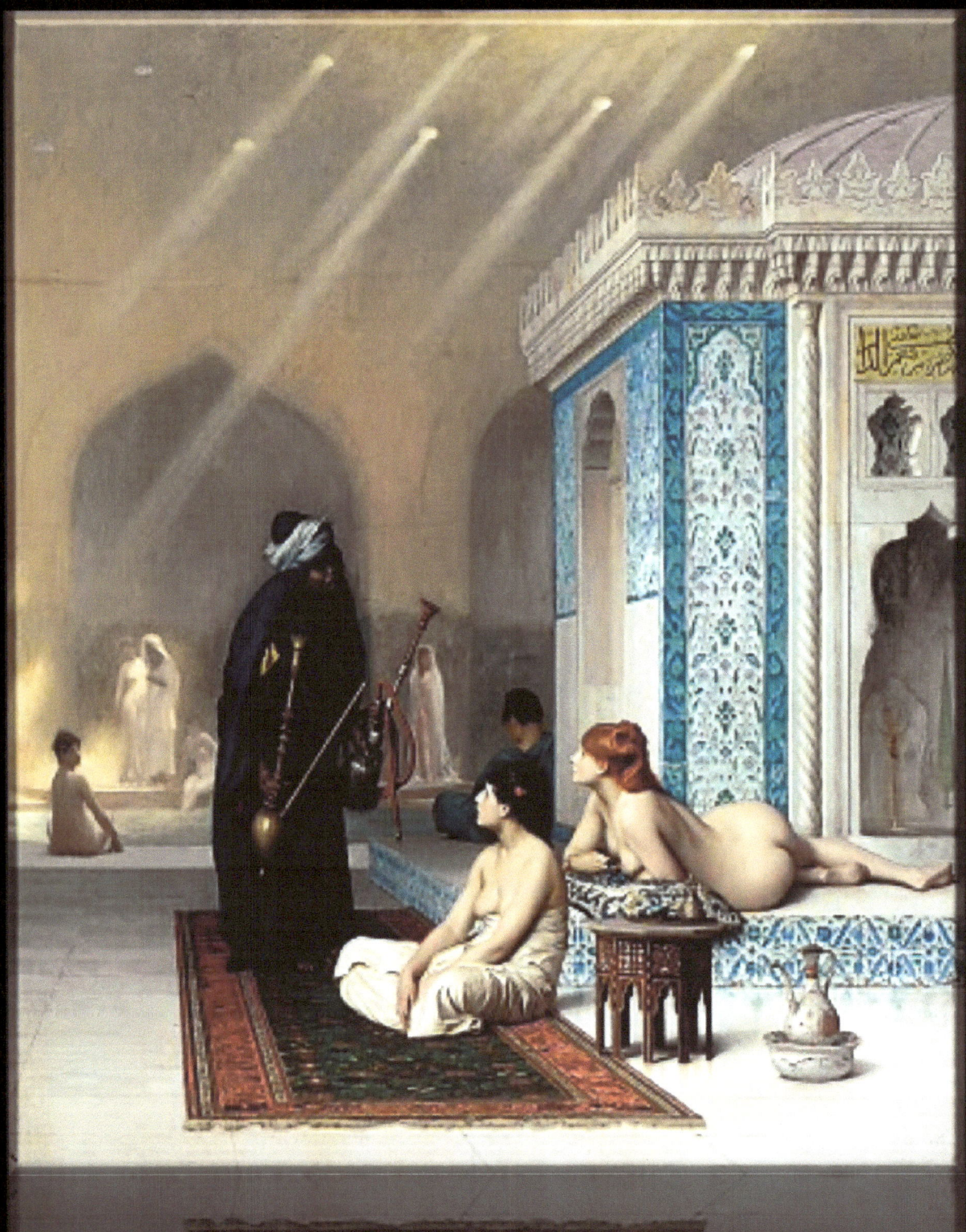

Pool in a Harem (Une piscine dans le harem) 1876 oil on canvas painting by French artist Jean-Leon Gerome

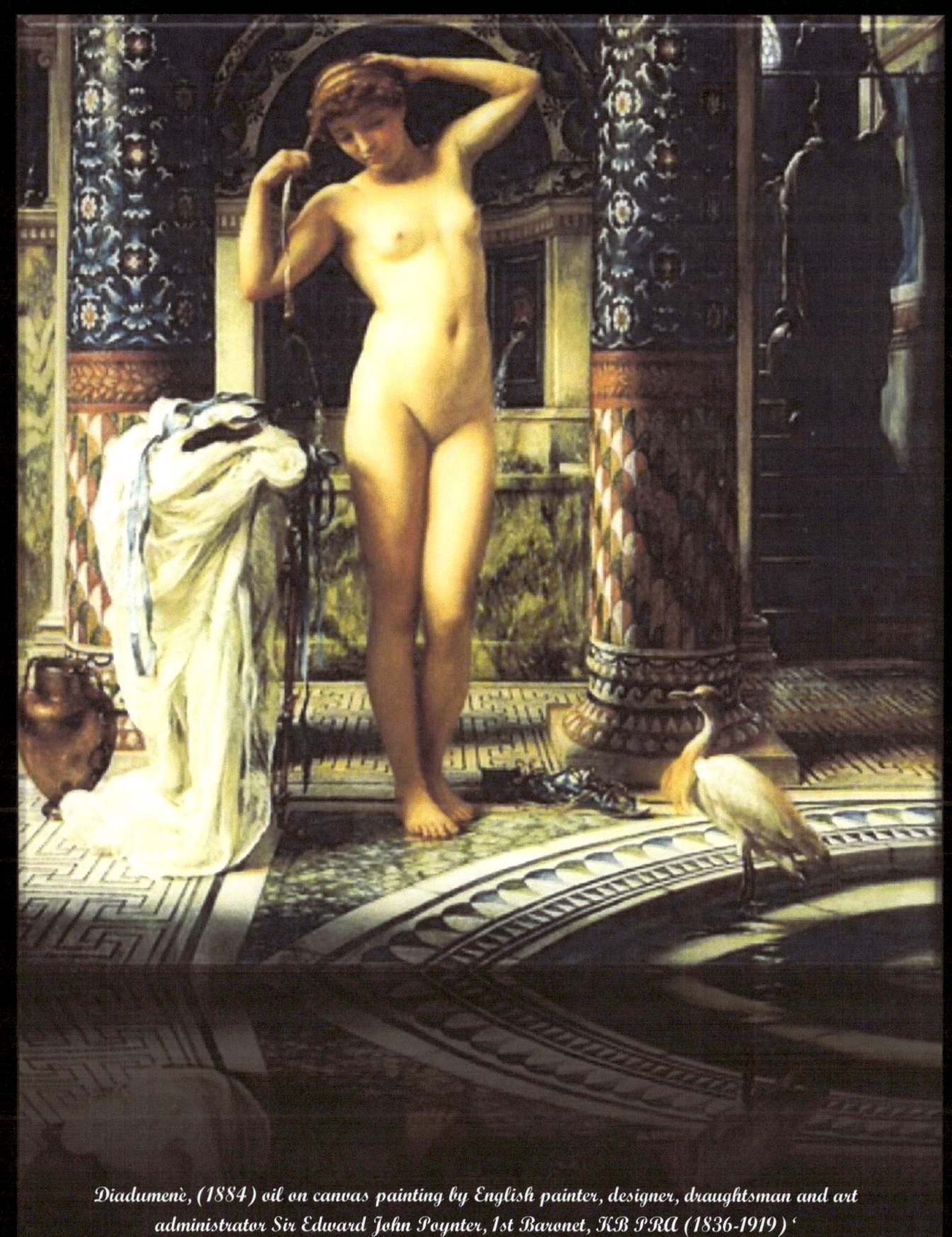

Diadumenè, (1884) oil on canvas painting by English painter, designer, draughtsman and art administrator Sir Edward John Poynter, 1st Baronet, KB PRA (1836-1919) '

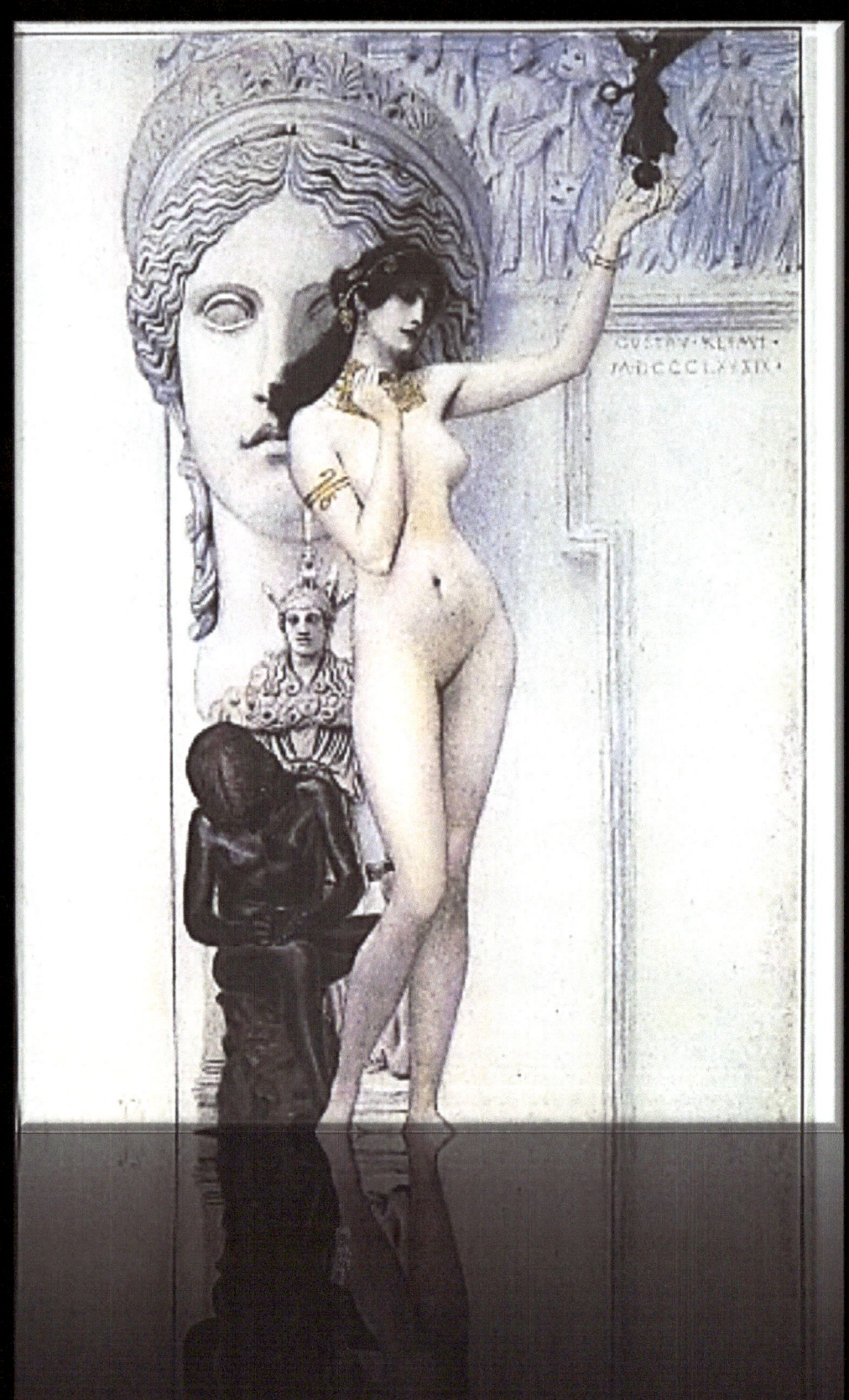

Allegory of sculpture' (Allegorie der Skulptur) an 1889 painting (signed towards the top right of the work as 'Gustav Klimt MDCCCLXXXIX', or 1889)

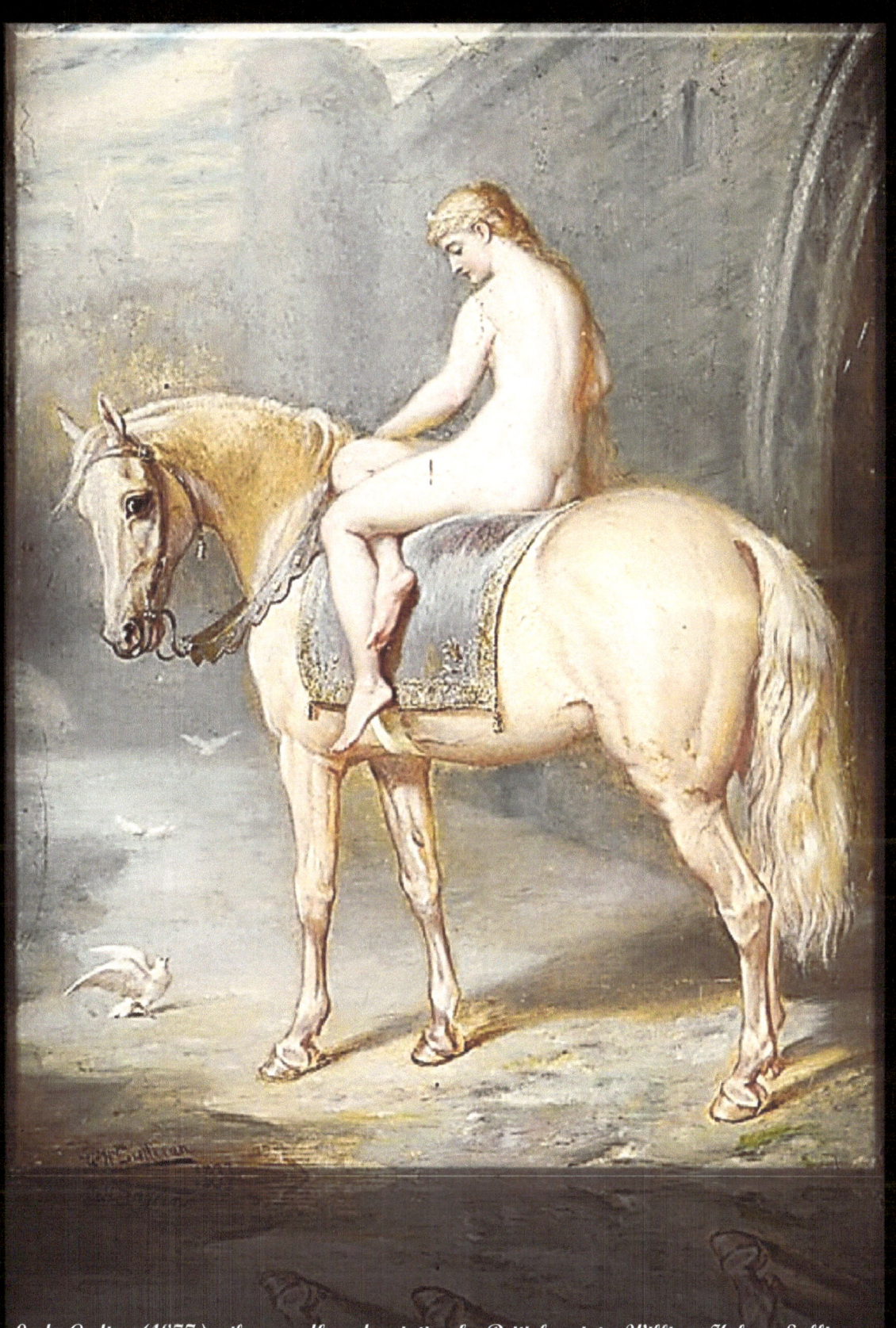

Lady Godiva (1877), oil on cardboard painting by British painter William Holmes Sullivan

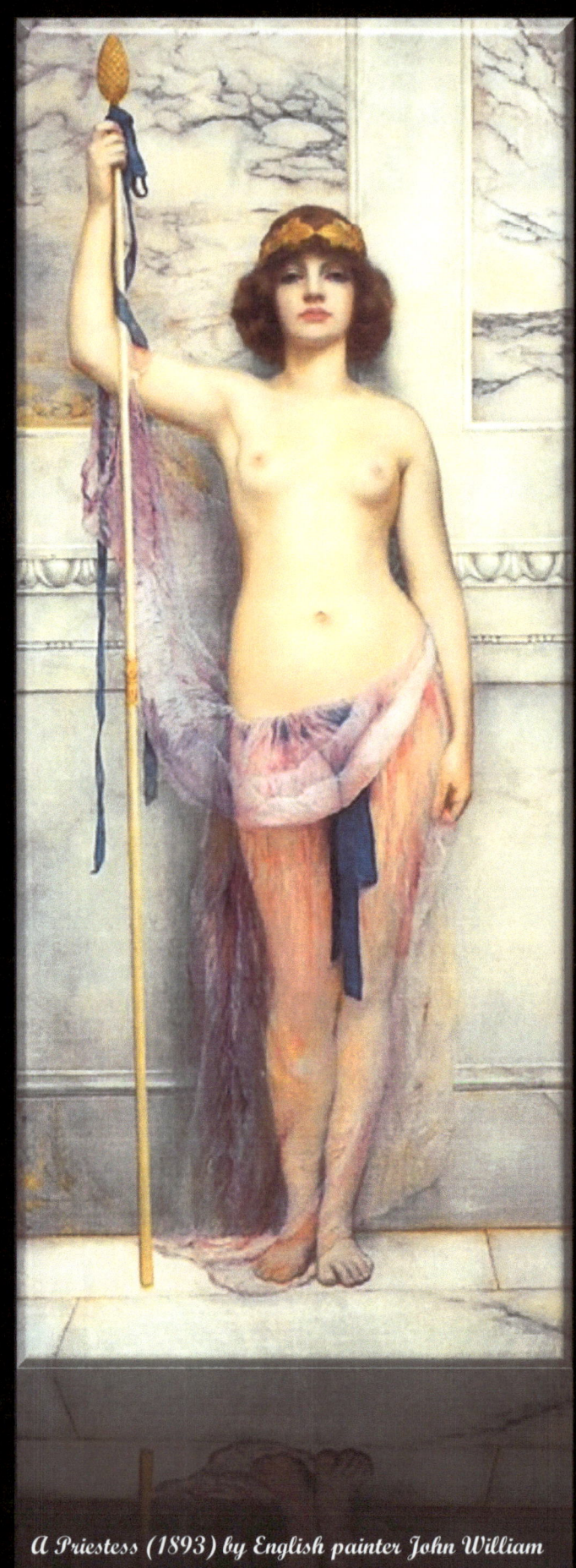

A Priestess (1893) by English painter John William

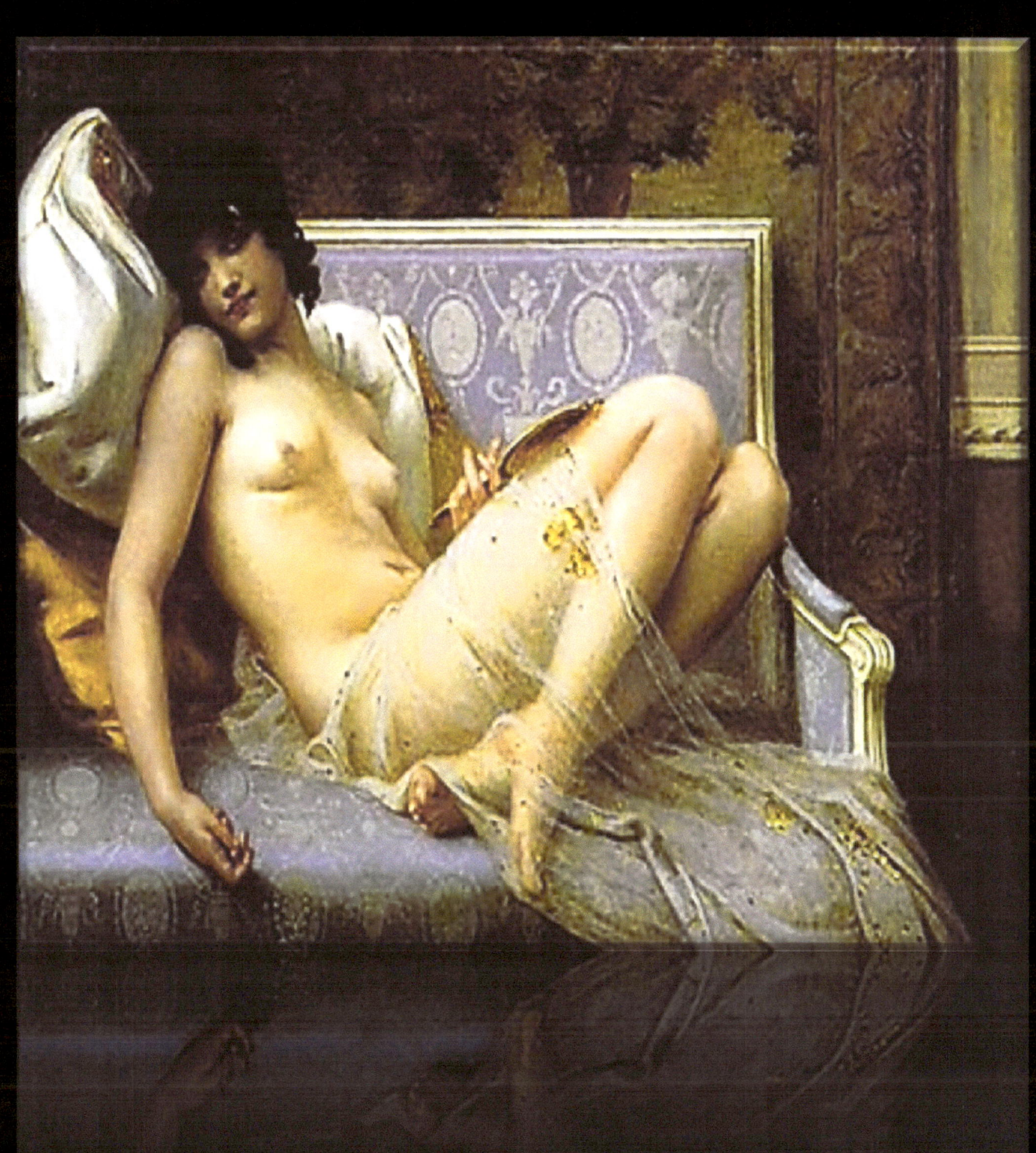

'Young woman on a settee' by French painter Guillaume Seignac (1870-1924), private collection.

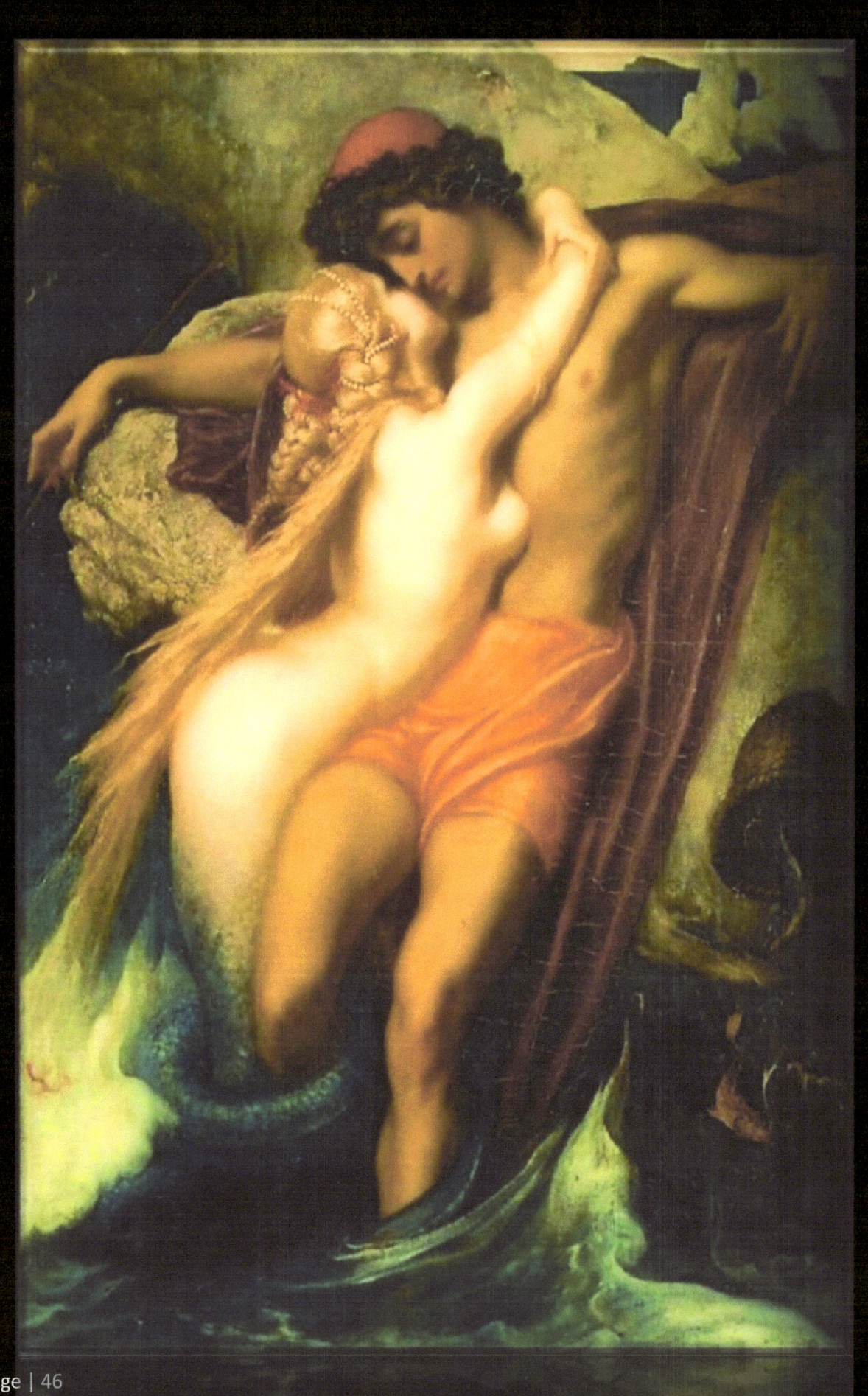

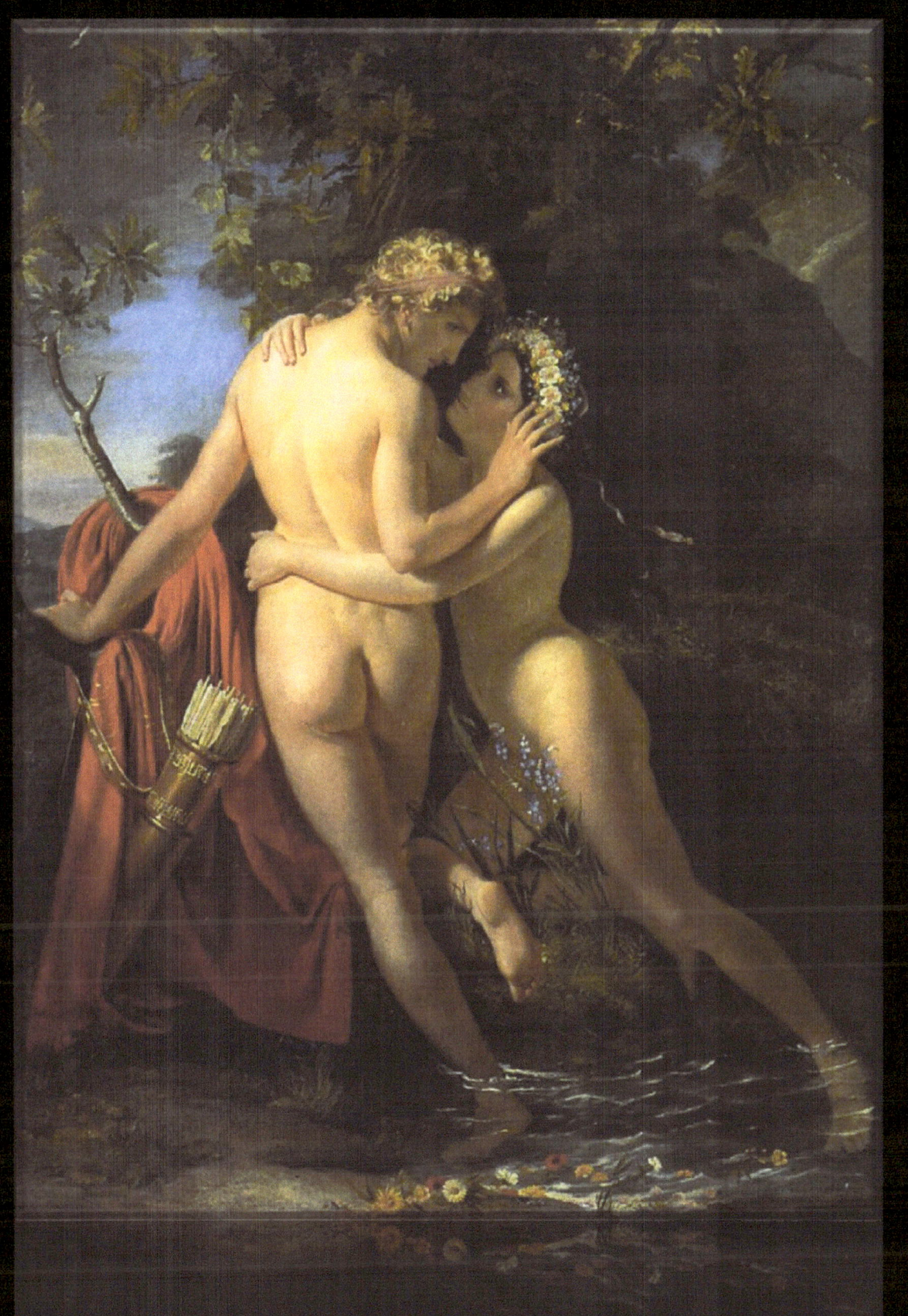

The Nymph Salmacis and Hermaphroditus (1828) by Belgian neo-classical painter François-Joseph Navez (1787-186

9).

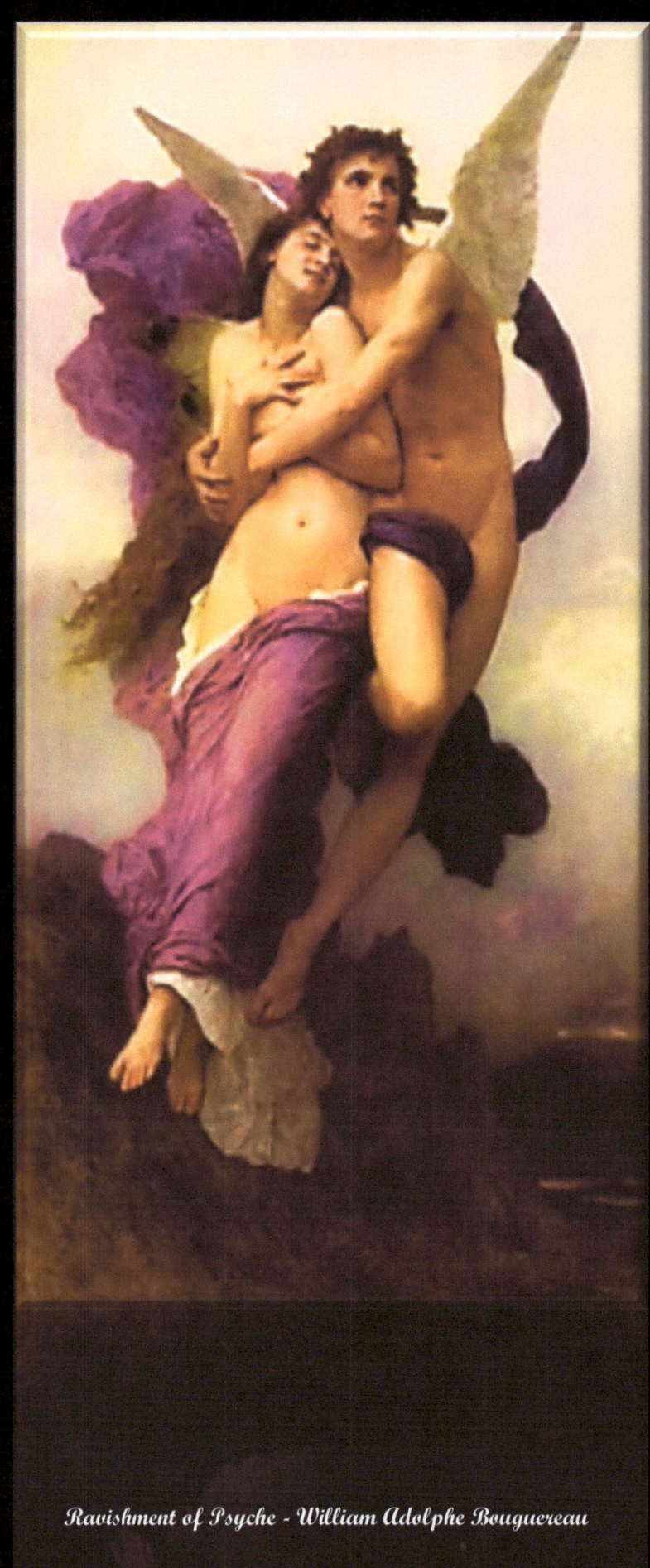

Ravishment of Psyche - William Adolphe Bouguereau

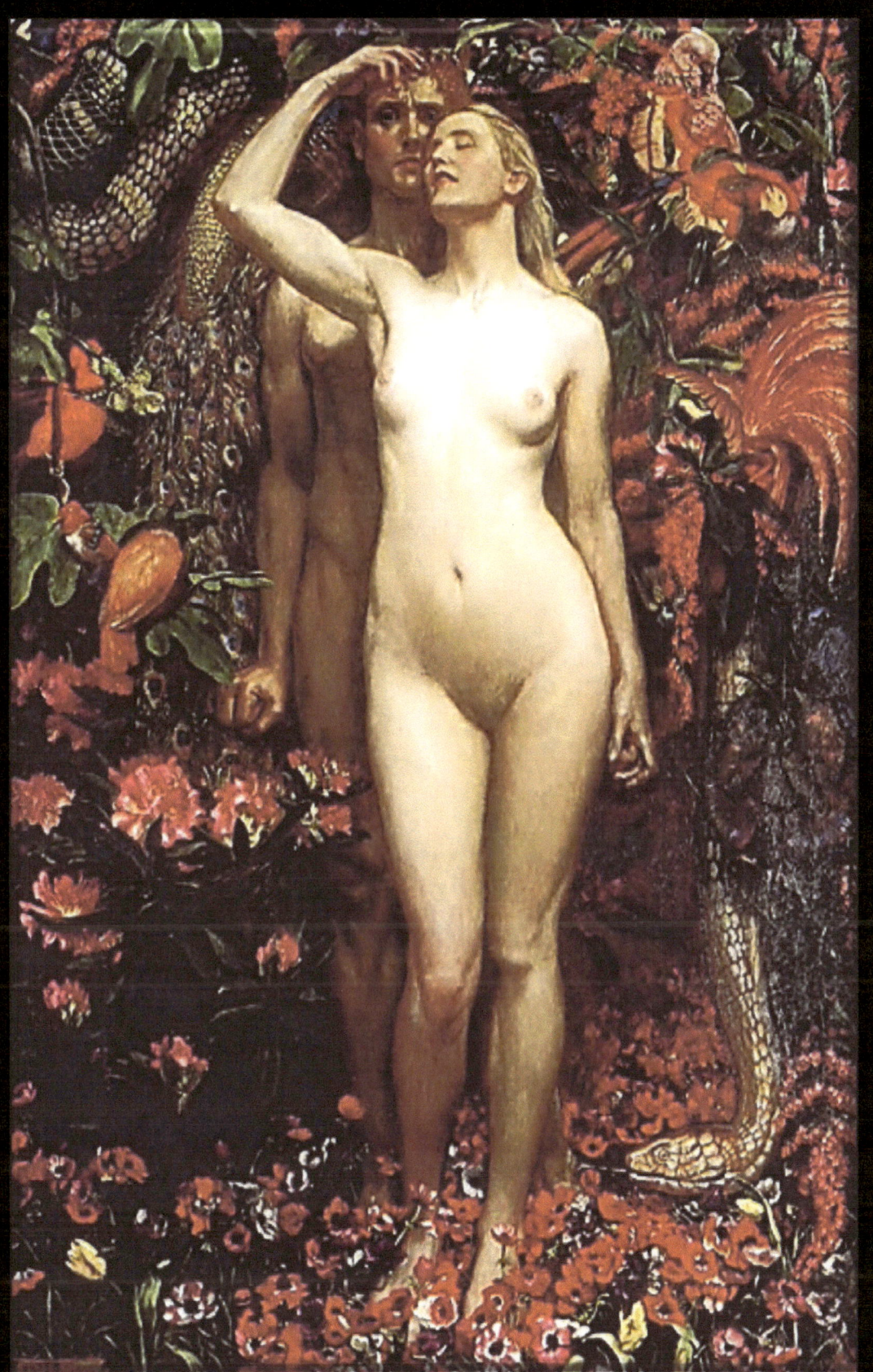

'The Woman The Man The Serpent', oil painting by Indian-born British painter, illustrator, designer and teacher Byam Shaw (1872-1919), depicting Adam, Eve and the serpent.

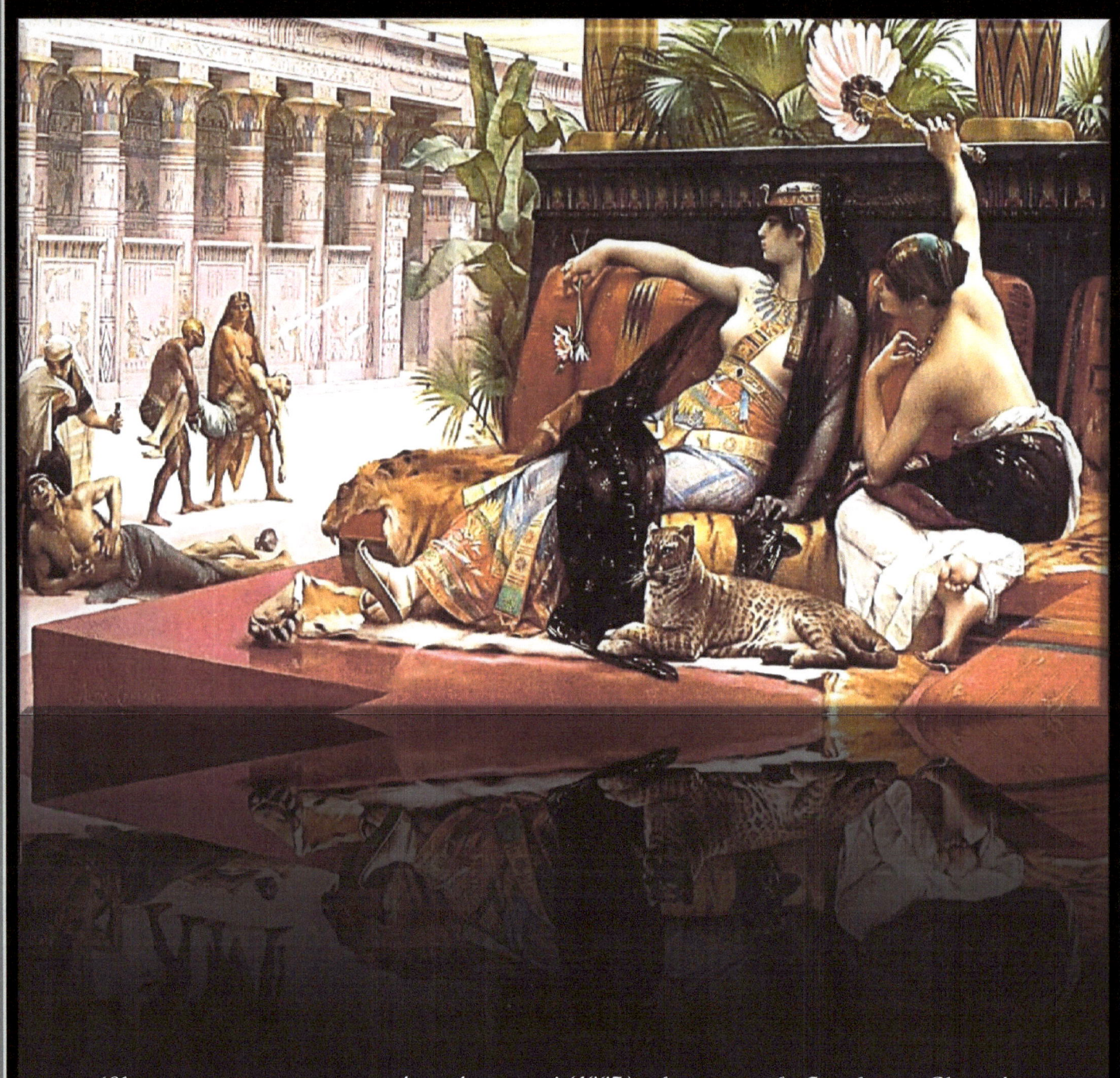

'Cleopatra testing poisons on condemned prisoners' (1887), oil on canvas, by French artist Alexandre Cabanel (1823-188

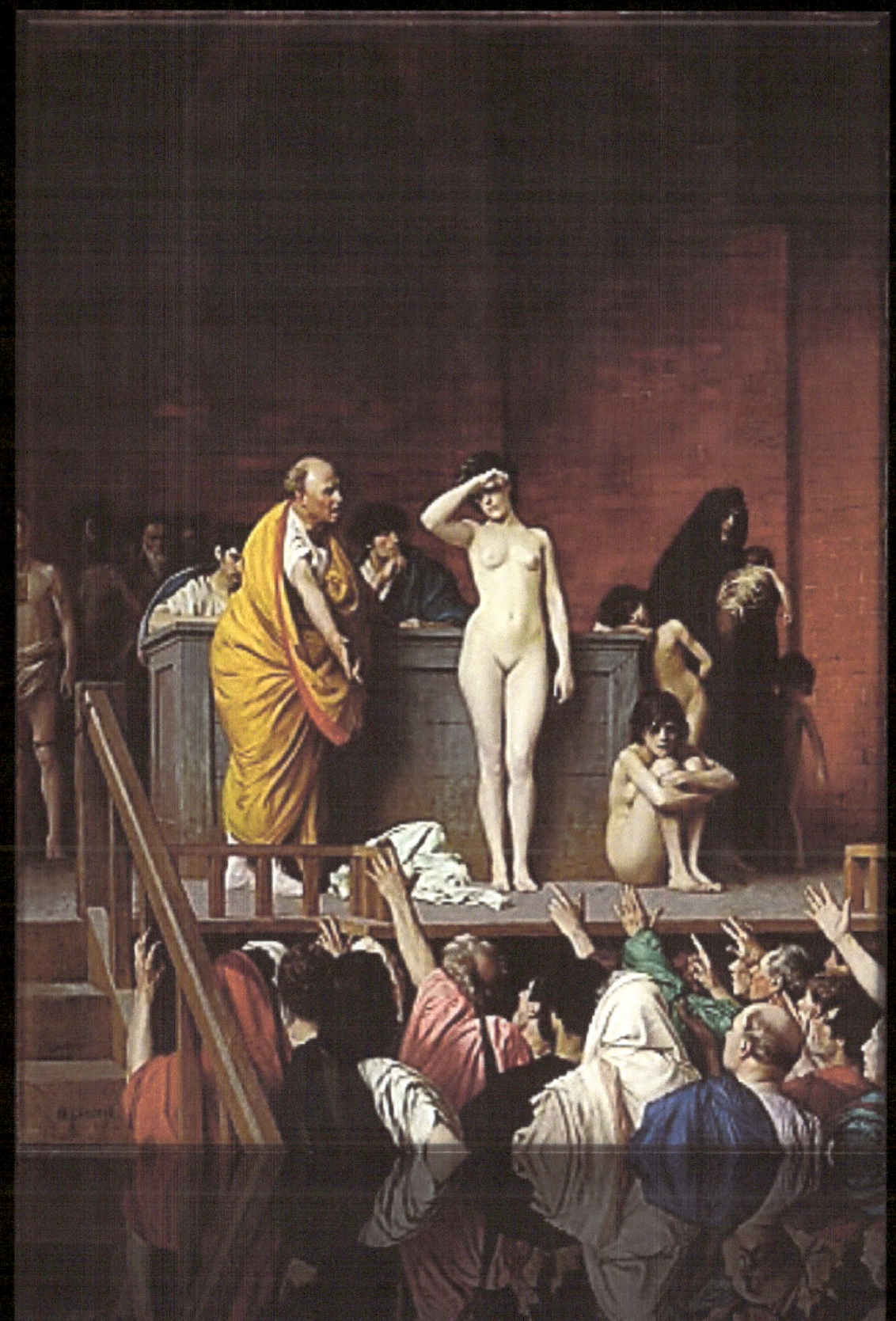

The Slave Market in Rome (Slave Auction) by French painter and sculptor Jean-Leon Gerome, a 1884 oil on canvas

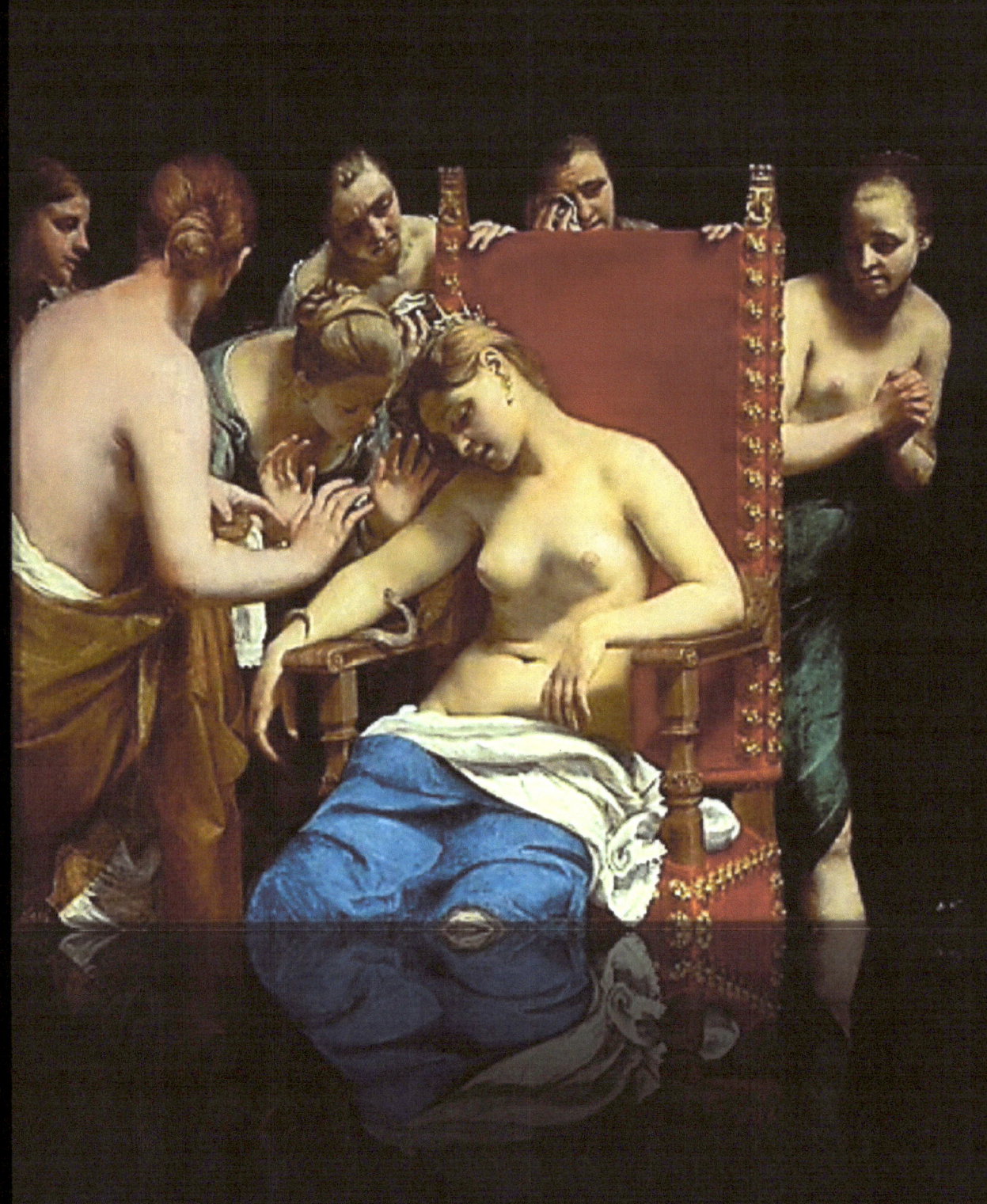

The Death of Cleopatra (1659) by Guido Cagnacci, oil on canvas

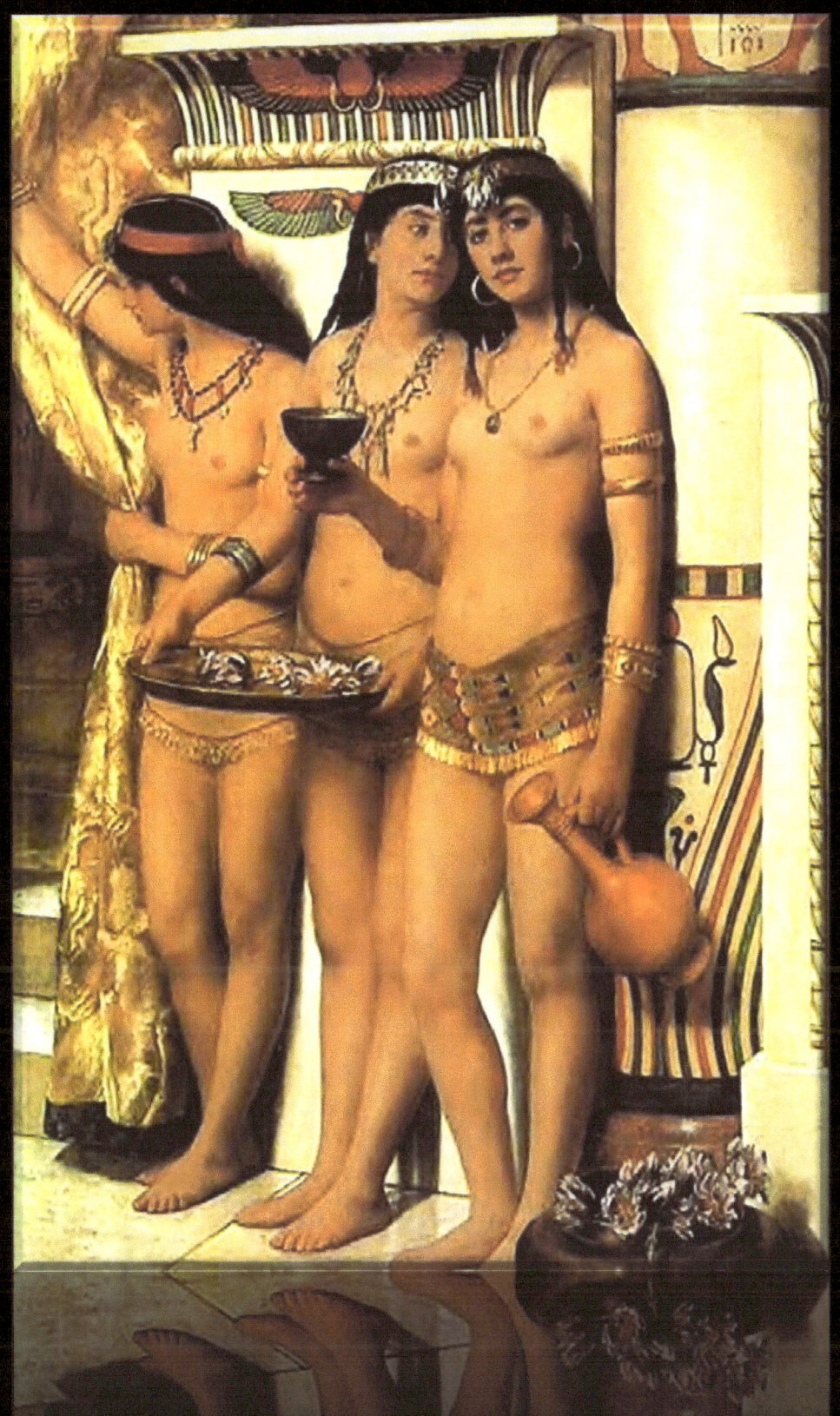

The Pharaoh's Handmaidens (1883) oil painting by British artist and author John Maler Collier.

Godward (1861-1922)

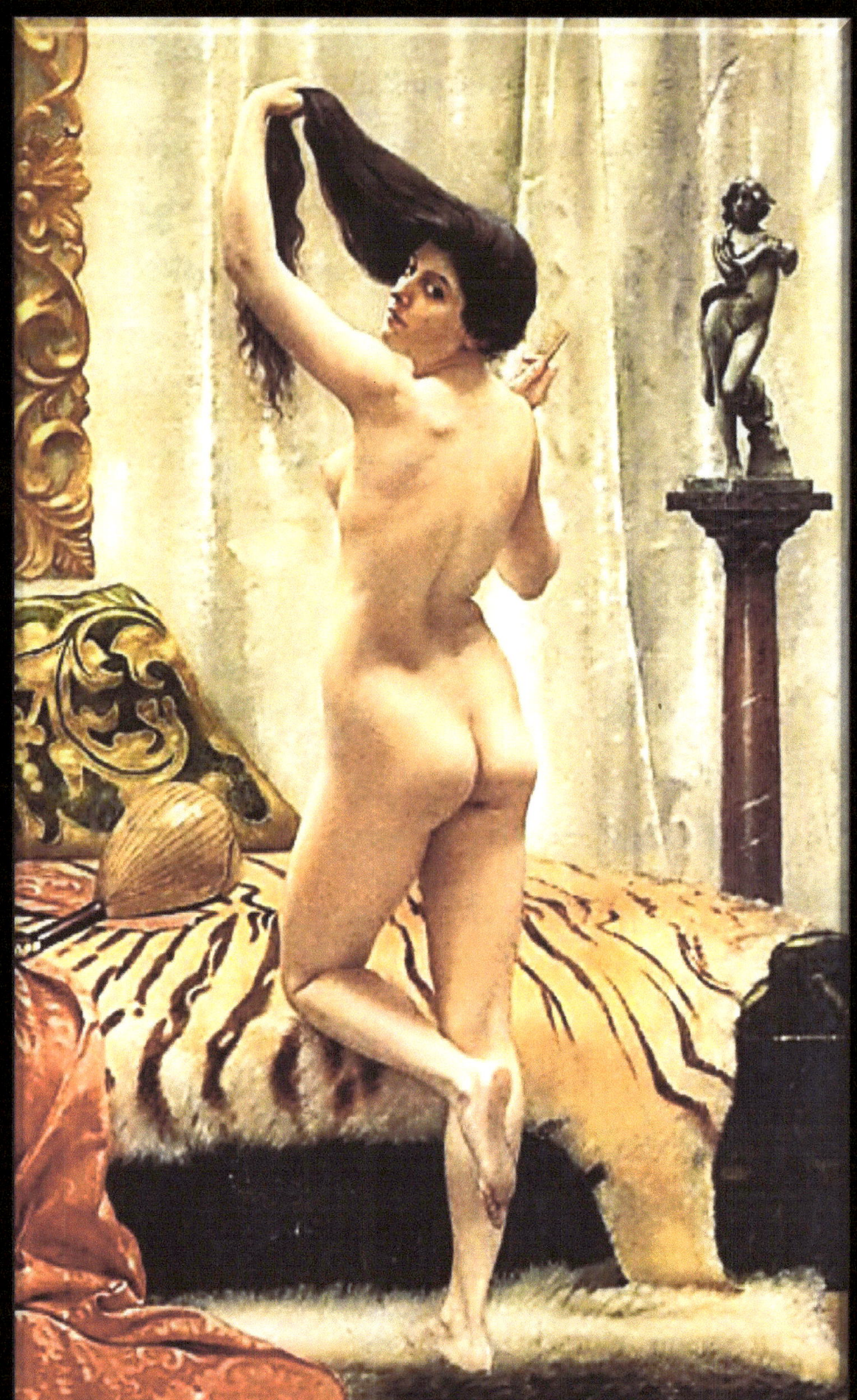

Before a Mirror (Devant un miroir), oil on canvas painting painted before 1912 by the English painter Robert Wiedeman Barrett Browning, also known as Pen Browning (1849-1912)

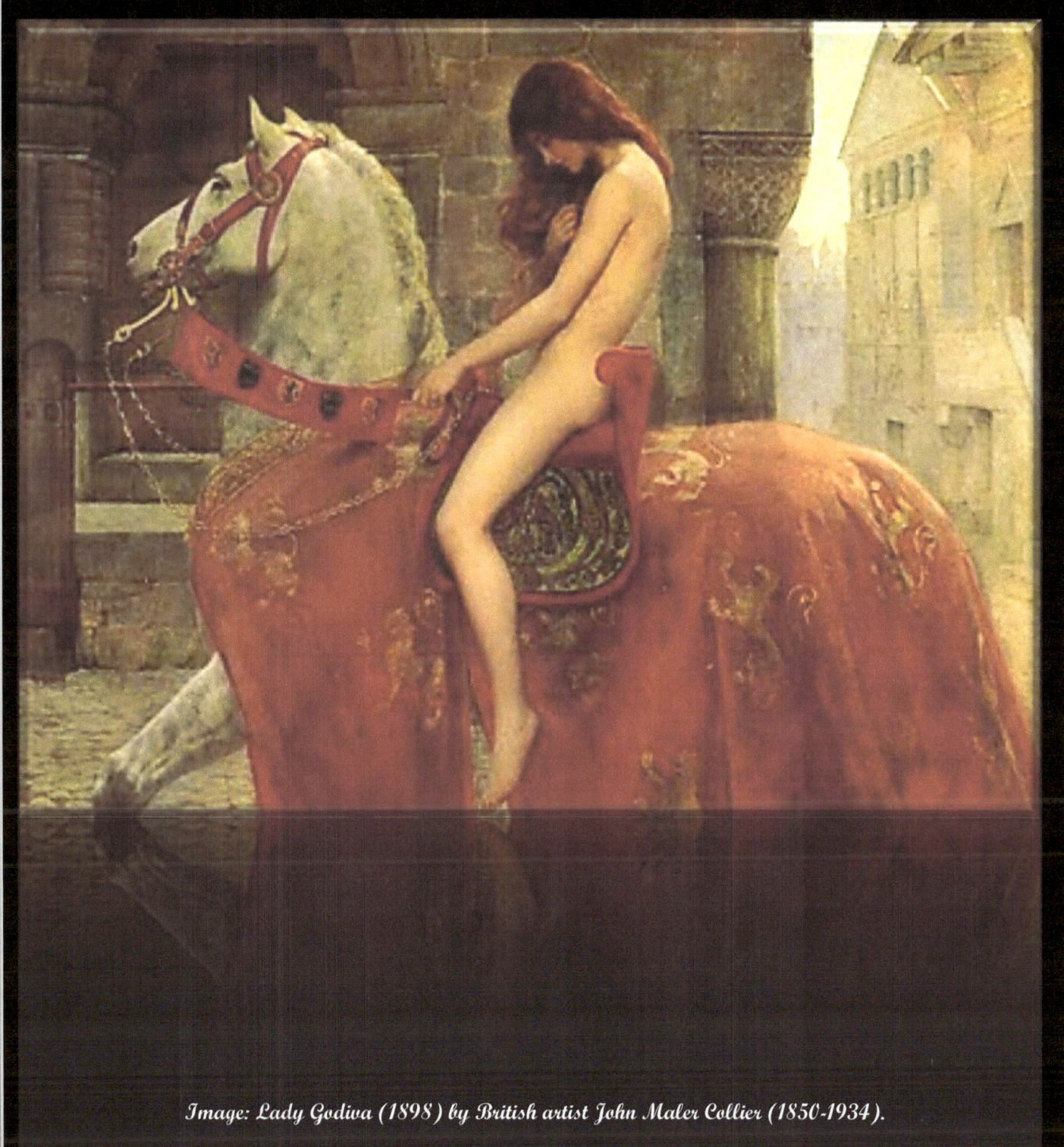

Image: Lady Godiva (1898) by British artist John Maler Collier (1850-1934).

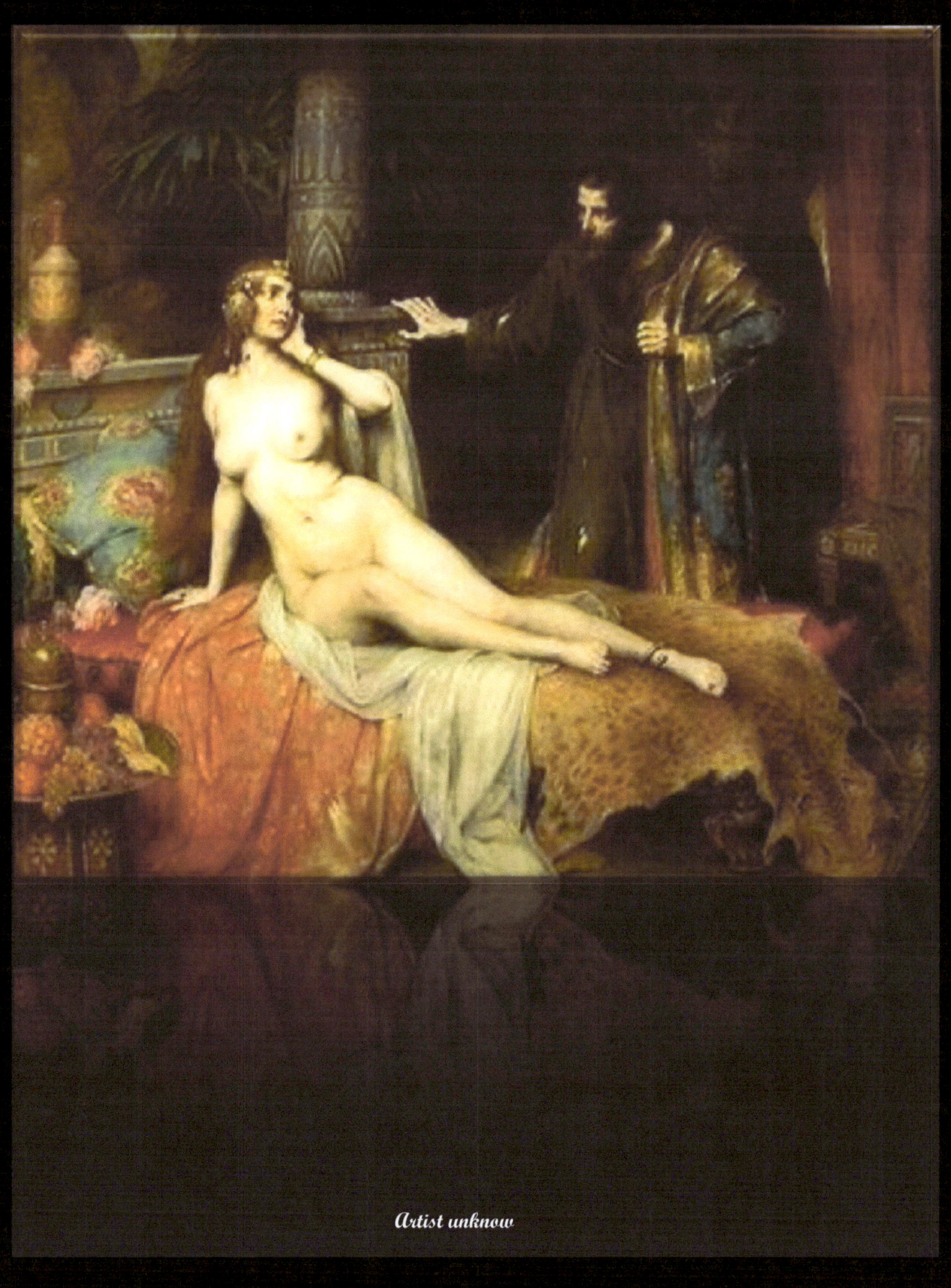

Artist unknow

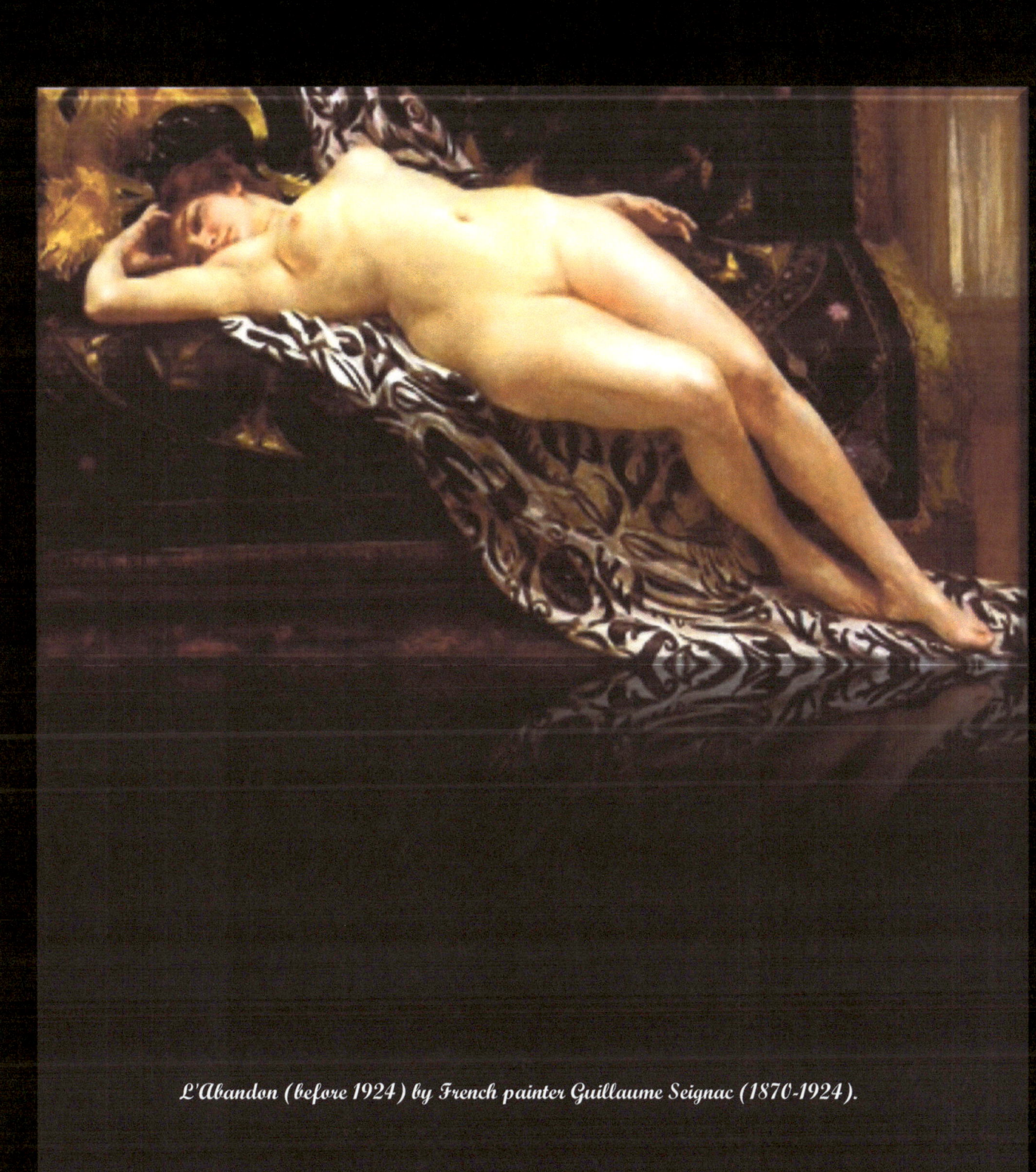

L'Abandon (before 1924) by French painter Guillaume Seignac (1870-1924).

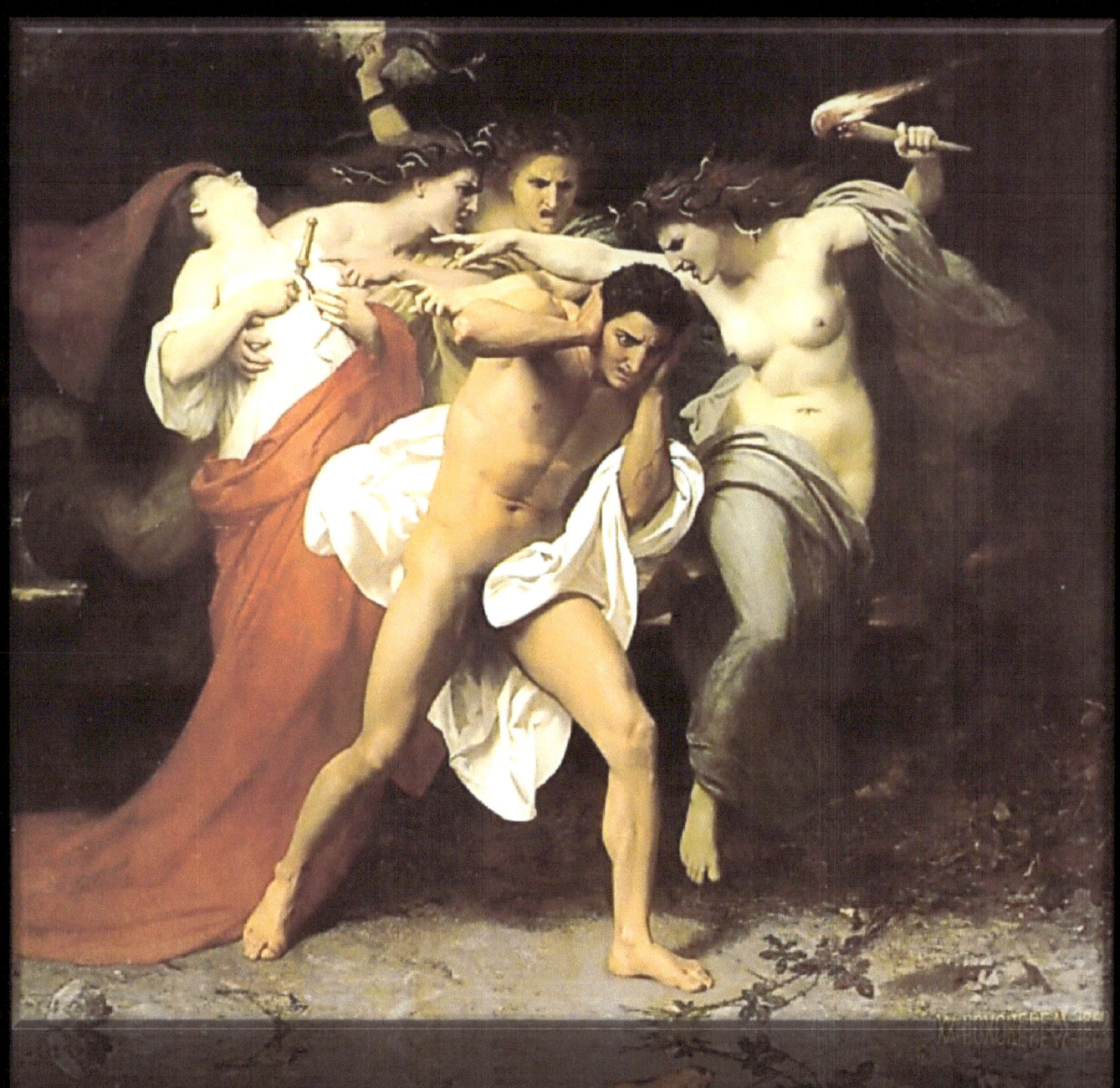

The Remorse of Orestes or Orestes Pursued by the Furies (alternate titles in other languages - French: Les Remords d'Oreste, Portuguese: O Remorso de Orestes, and Spanish: El Remordimiento de Orestes), a 1862 oil on canvas painting by William-Adolphe Bouguereau (1825-1905),

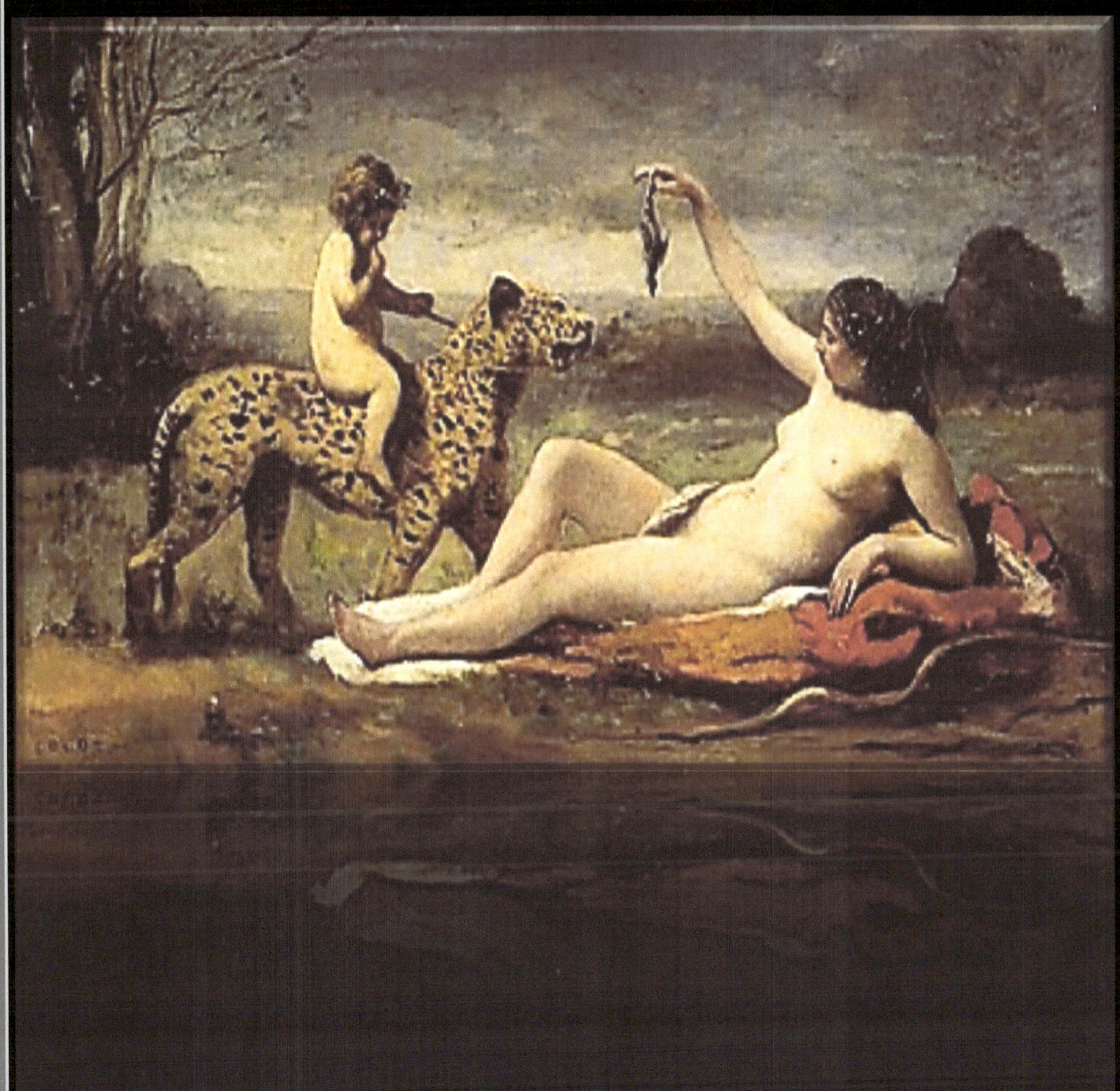

Bacchante with a Panther, oil painting on canvas painting by French landscape painter Jean-Baptiste Camille Corot., Jean-Baptiste Camille Corot, born in Paris on 16 July 1796

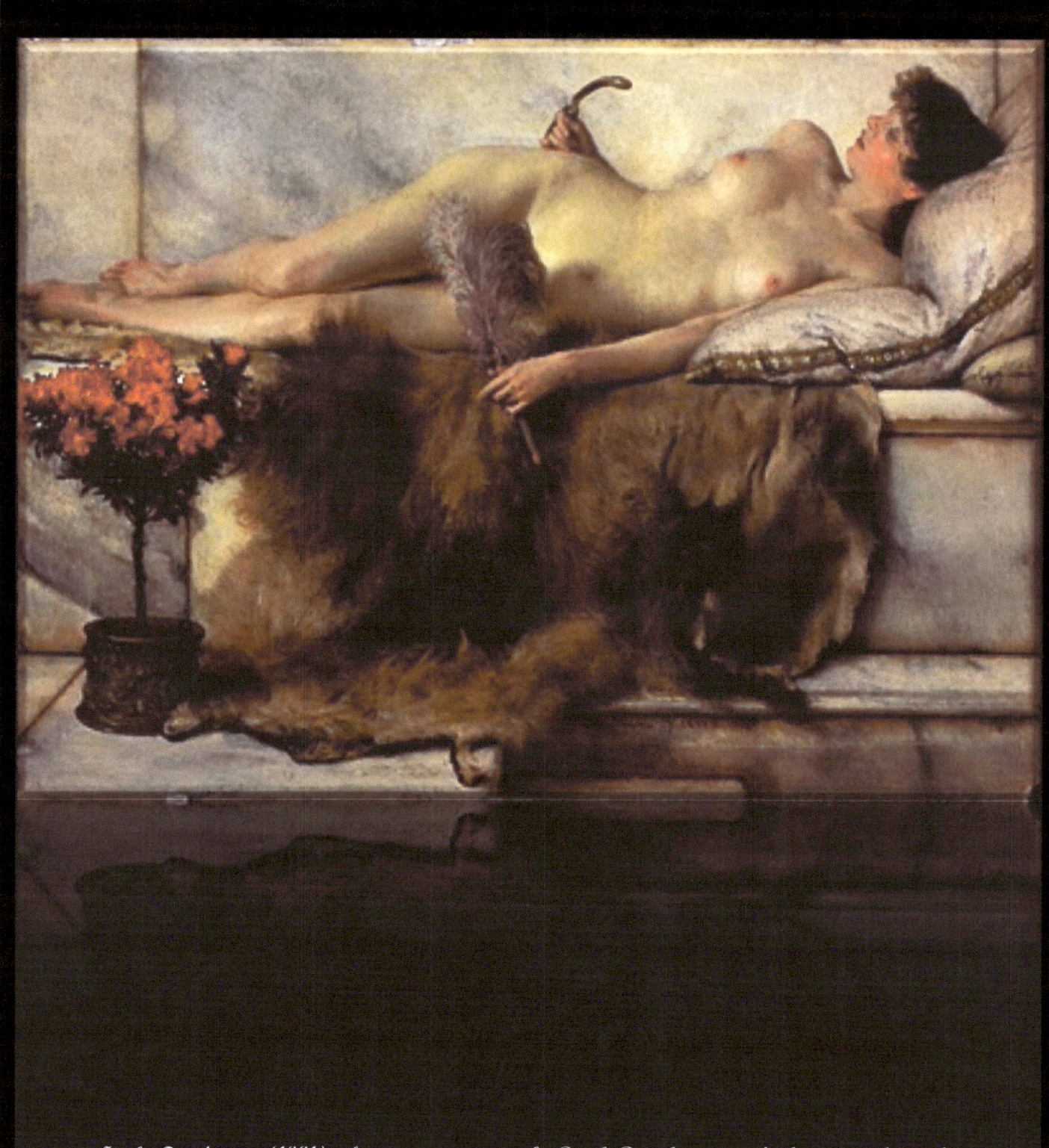

In the Tepidarium (1881), oil on canvas painting by Dutch-British painter, draftsman, etcher and illustrator Lawrence Alma Tadema (also spelled as Lourens | Laurens Alma Tadema, 1836-1912)

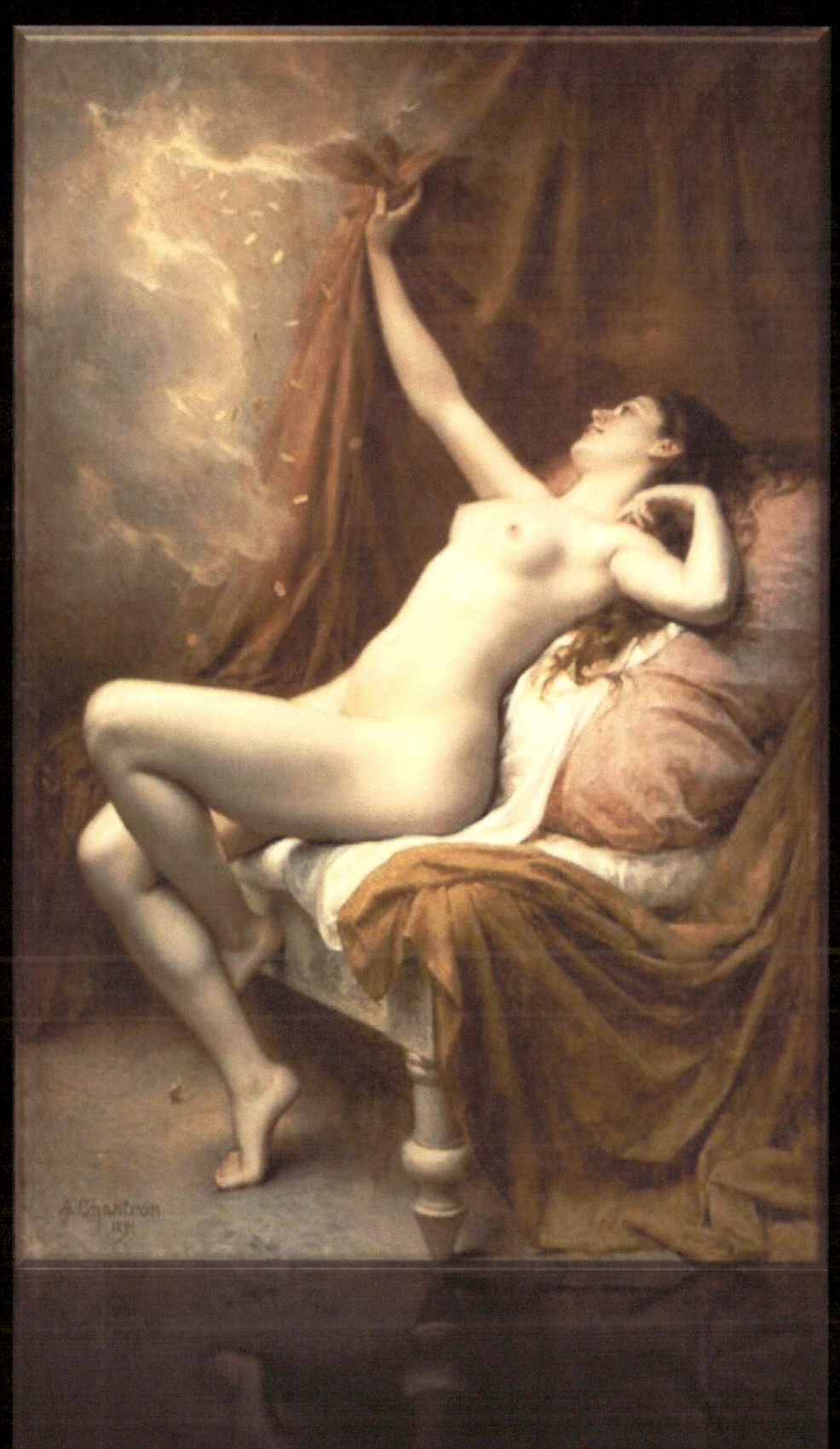

Danae (1891) oil painting by French painter and photographer Alexandre Jacques Chantron (1842-1918)

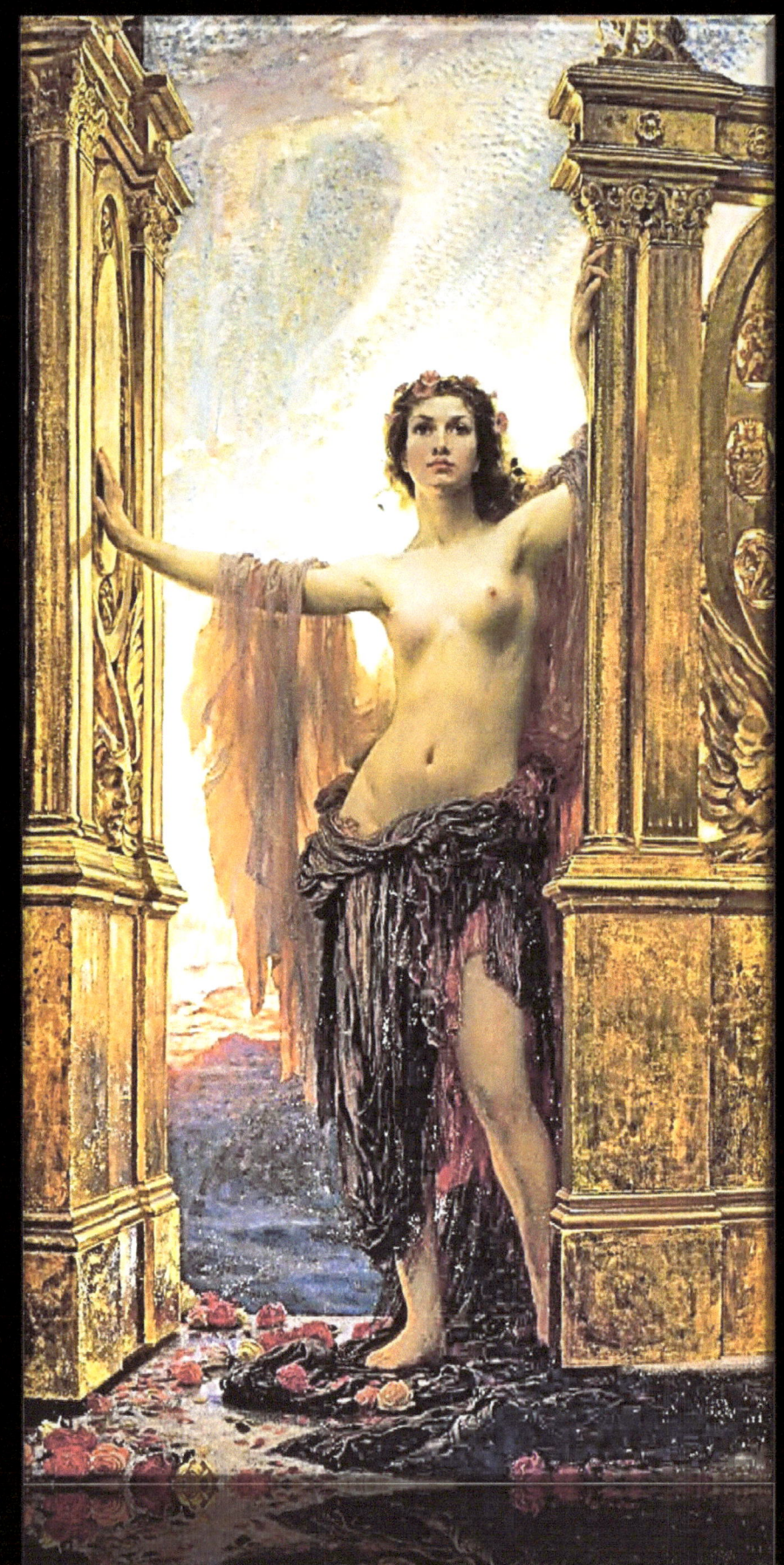

The Gates of Dawn (1900), oil painting by Herbert James Draper (1863-1920)

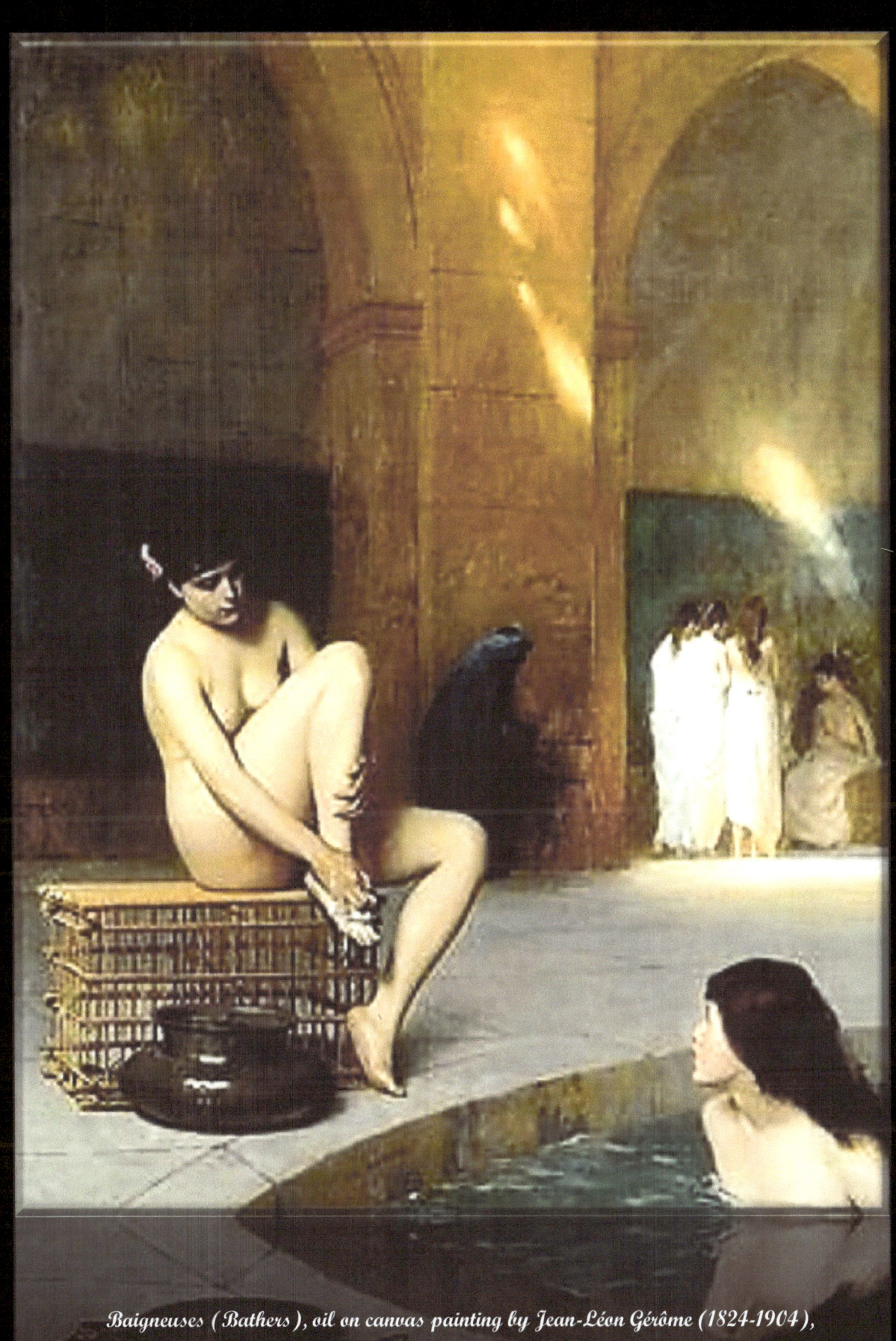

Baigneuses (Bathers), oil on canvas painting by Jean-Léon Gérôme (1824-1904),

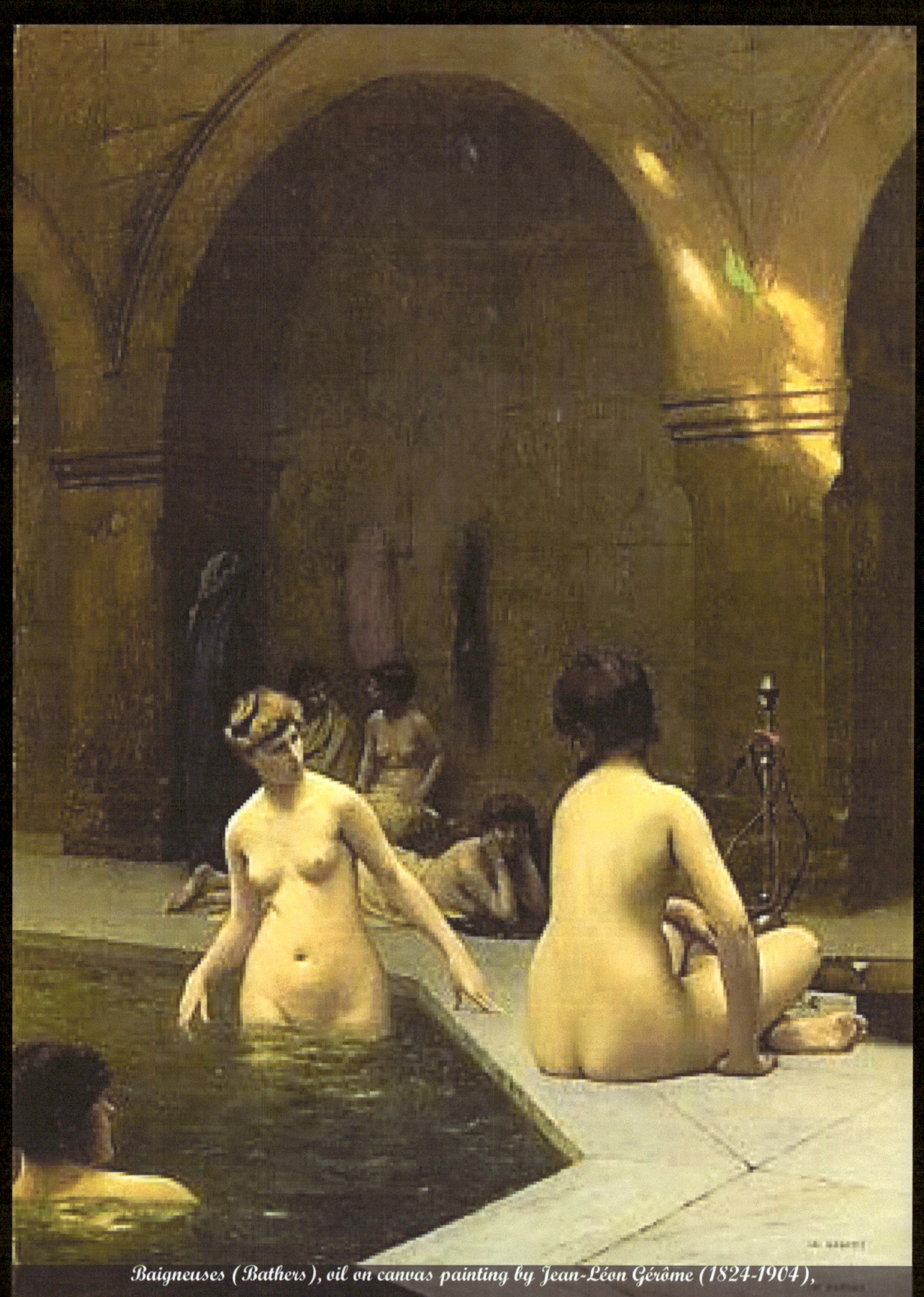

Baigneuses (Bathers), oil on canvas painting by Jean-Léon Gérôme (1824-1904),

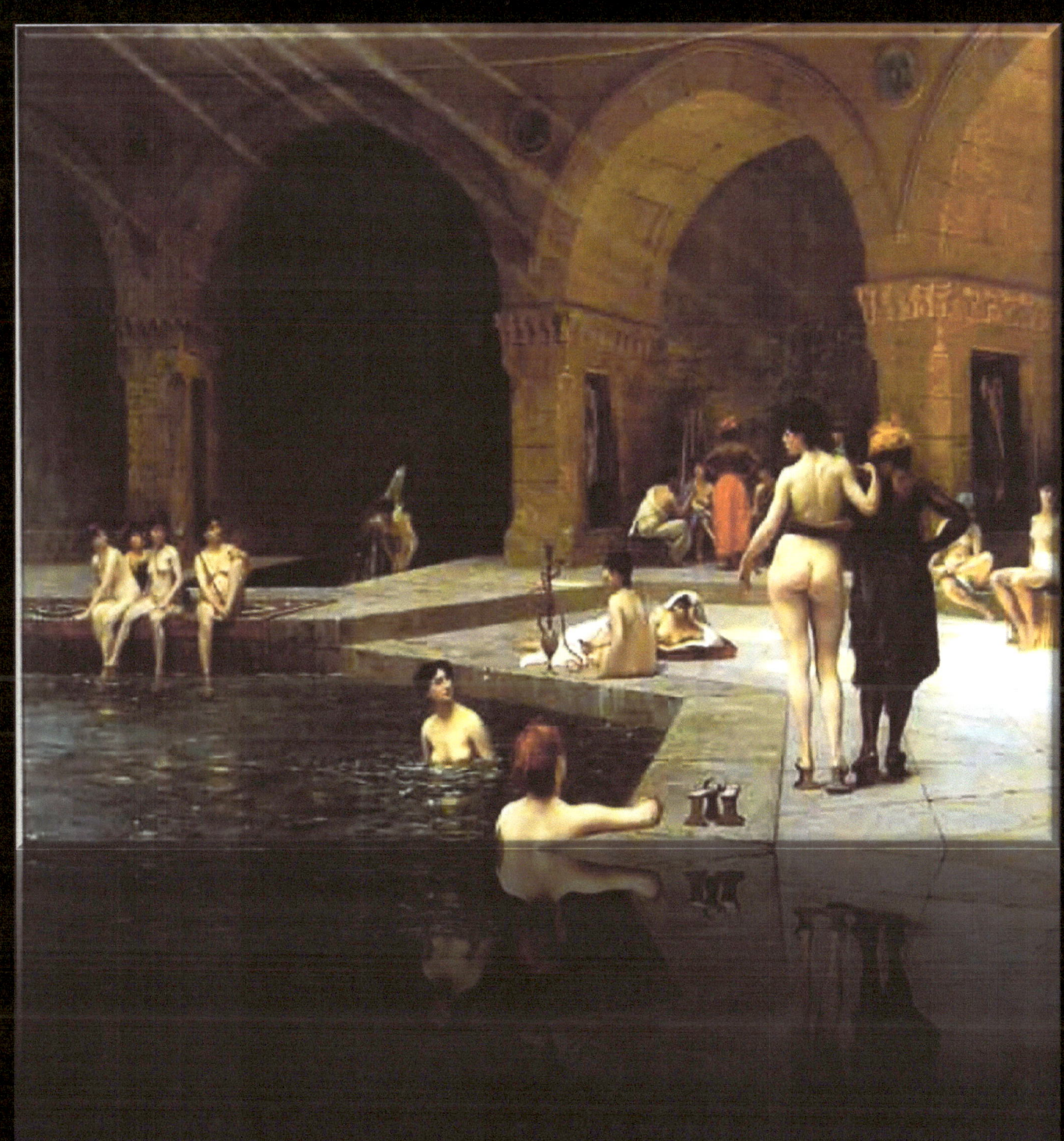

Harem Women Bathing', painting by French painter and sculptor Jean-Leon Gerome.

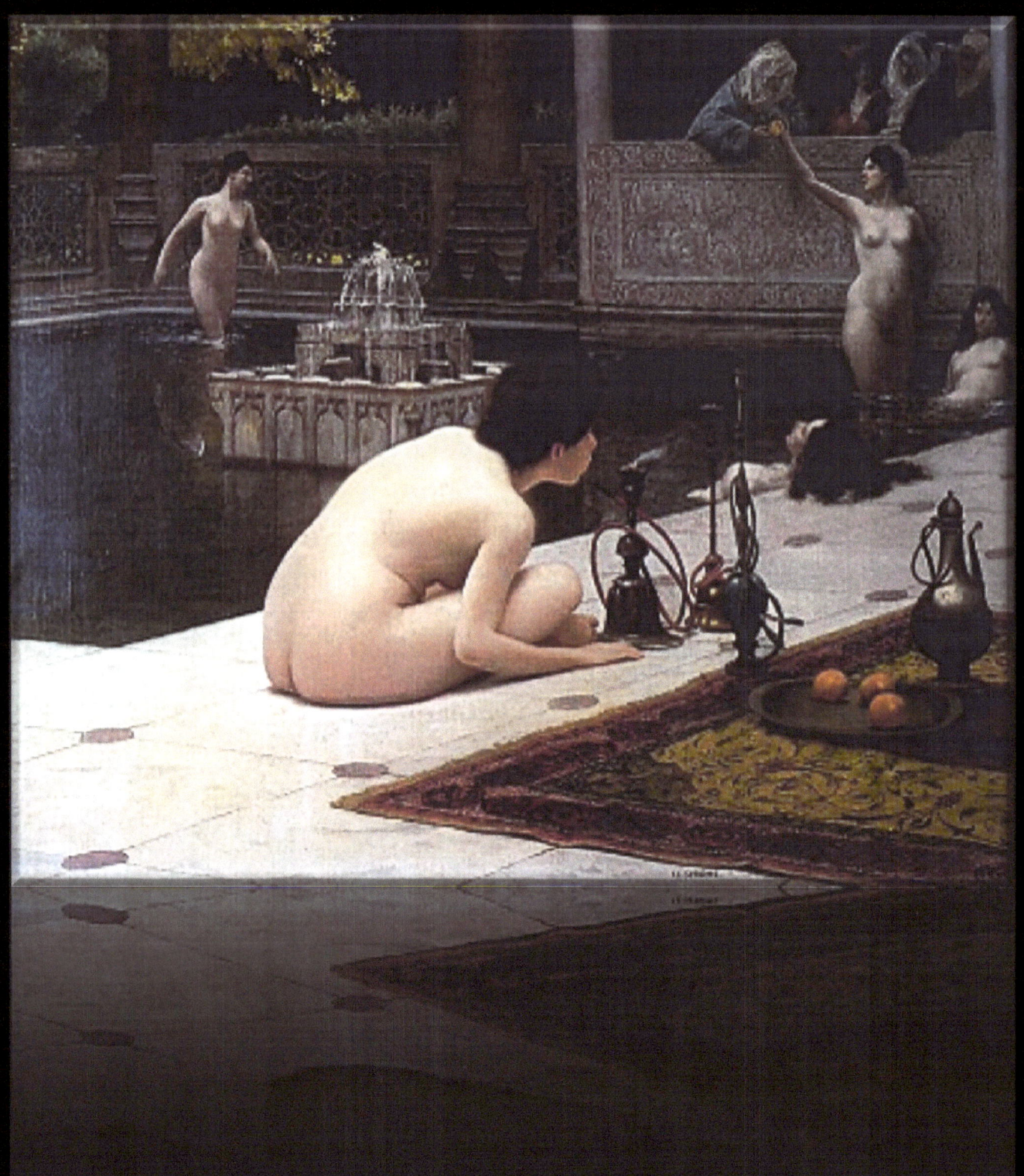

The Hookah Lighter (1898), oil on canvas painting by French painter and sculptor Jean-Leon Gerome.

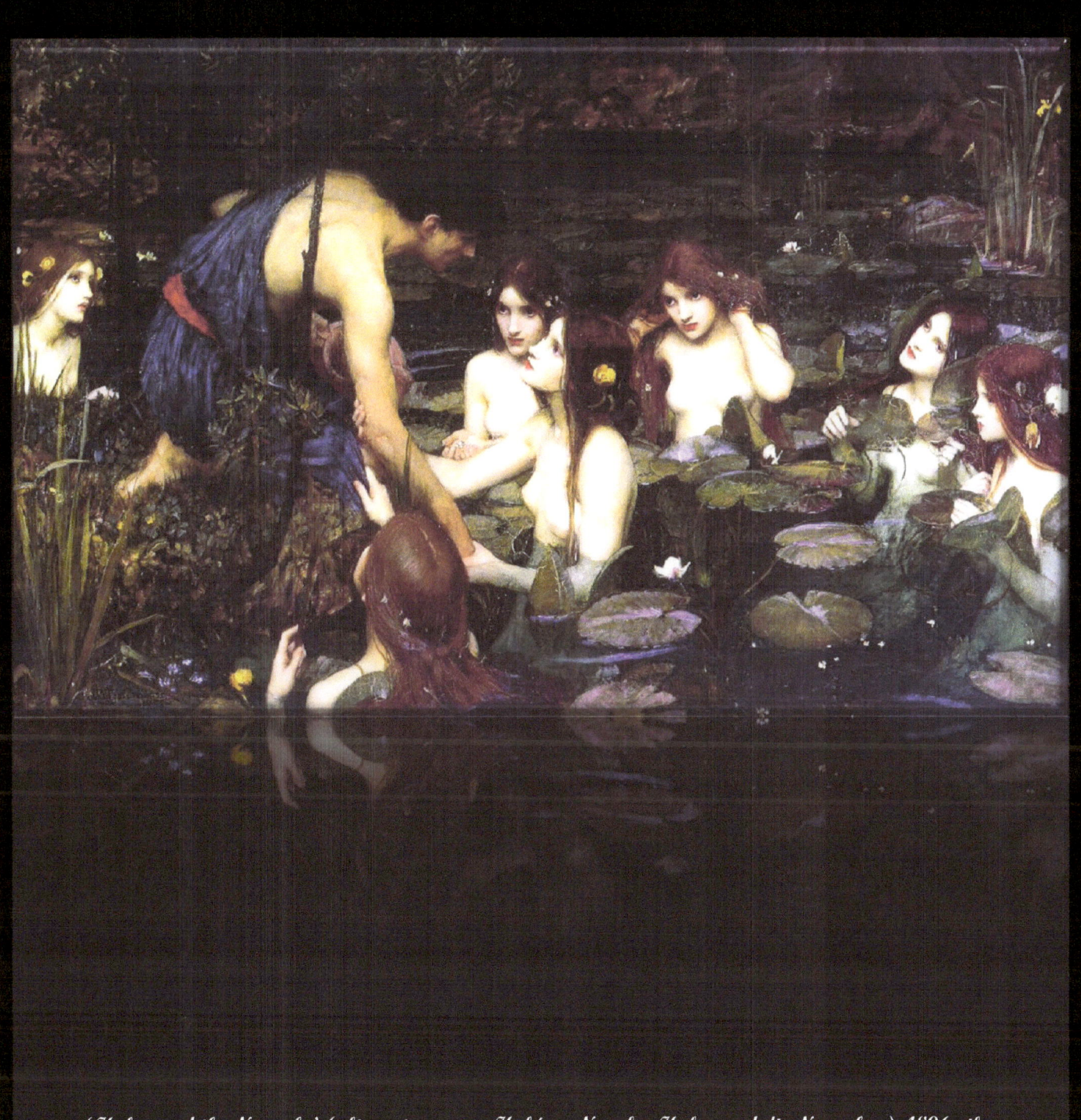

'Hylas and the Nymphs' (alternate names: Hylás a Nymfy, Hylas und die Nymphen), 1896 oil on canvas painting by British painter John William Waterhouse (1849-1917)

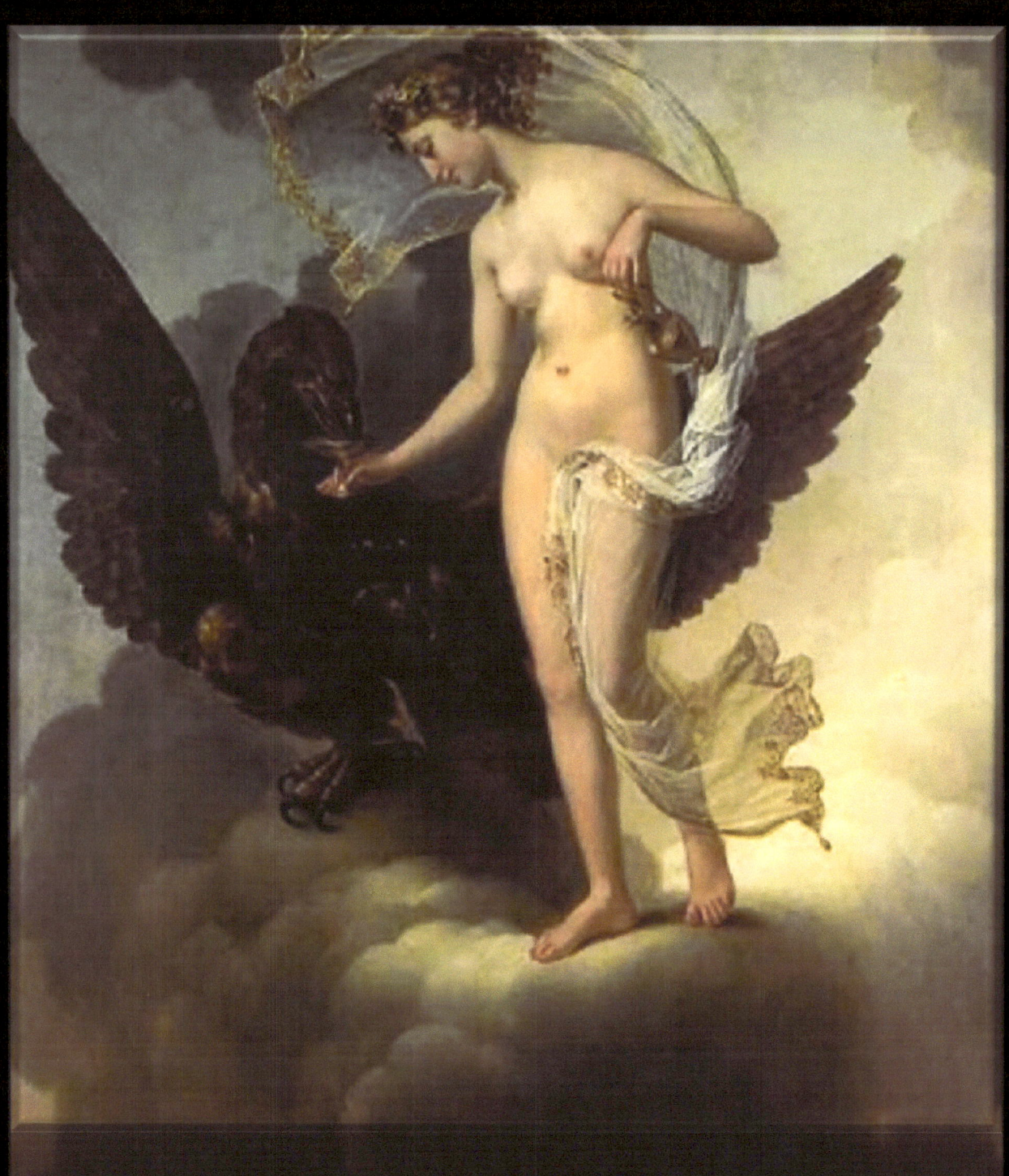

Portrait of Hebe (1826), oil on canvas painting by Charles Picqué (1799-1869),

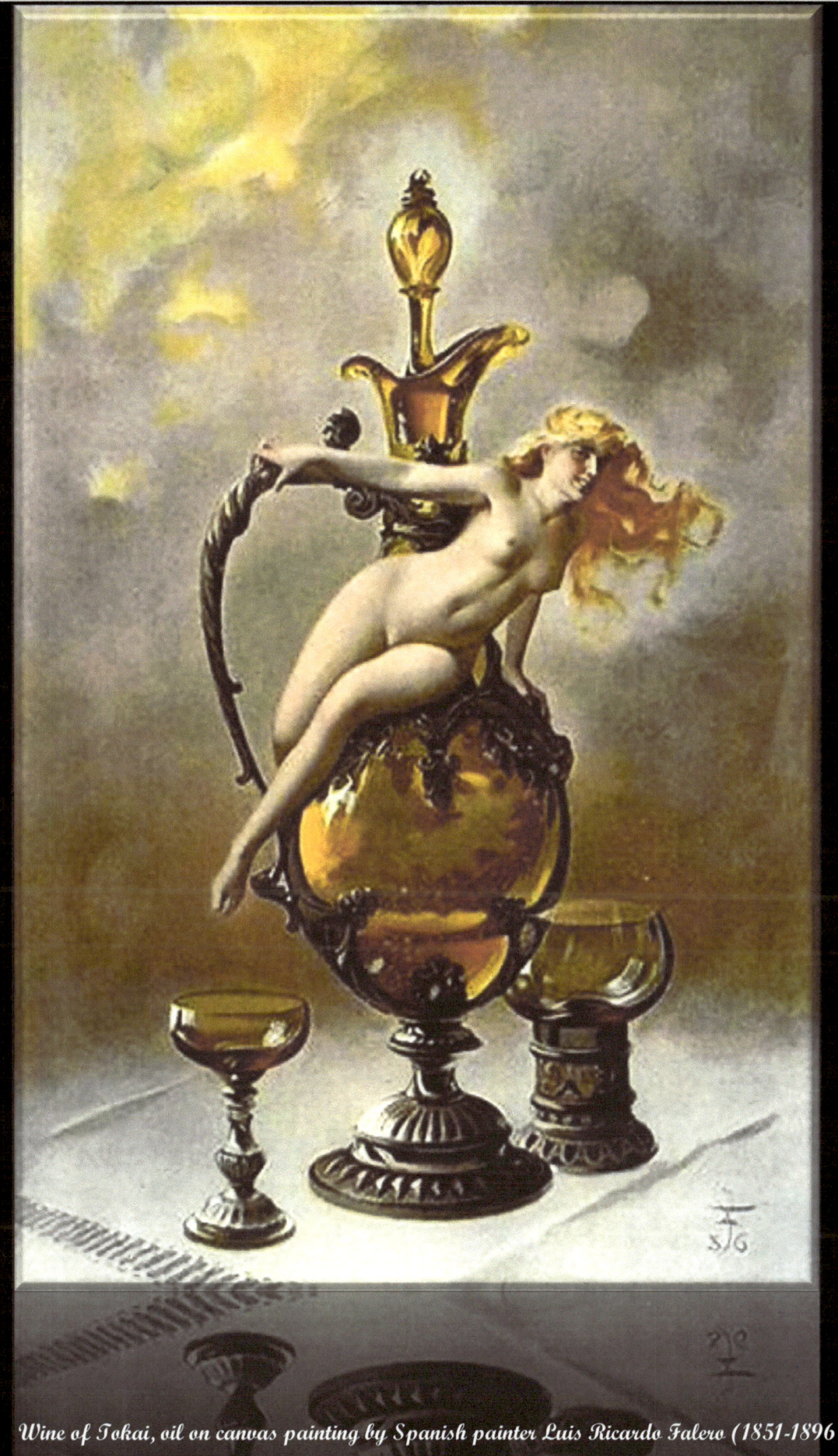

Wine of Tokai, oil on canvas painting by Spanish painter Luis Ricardo Falero (1851-1896

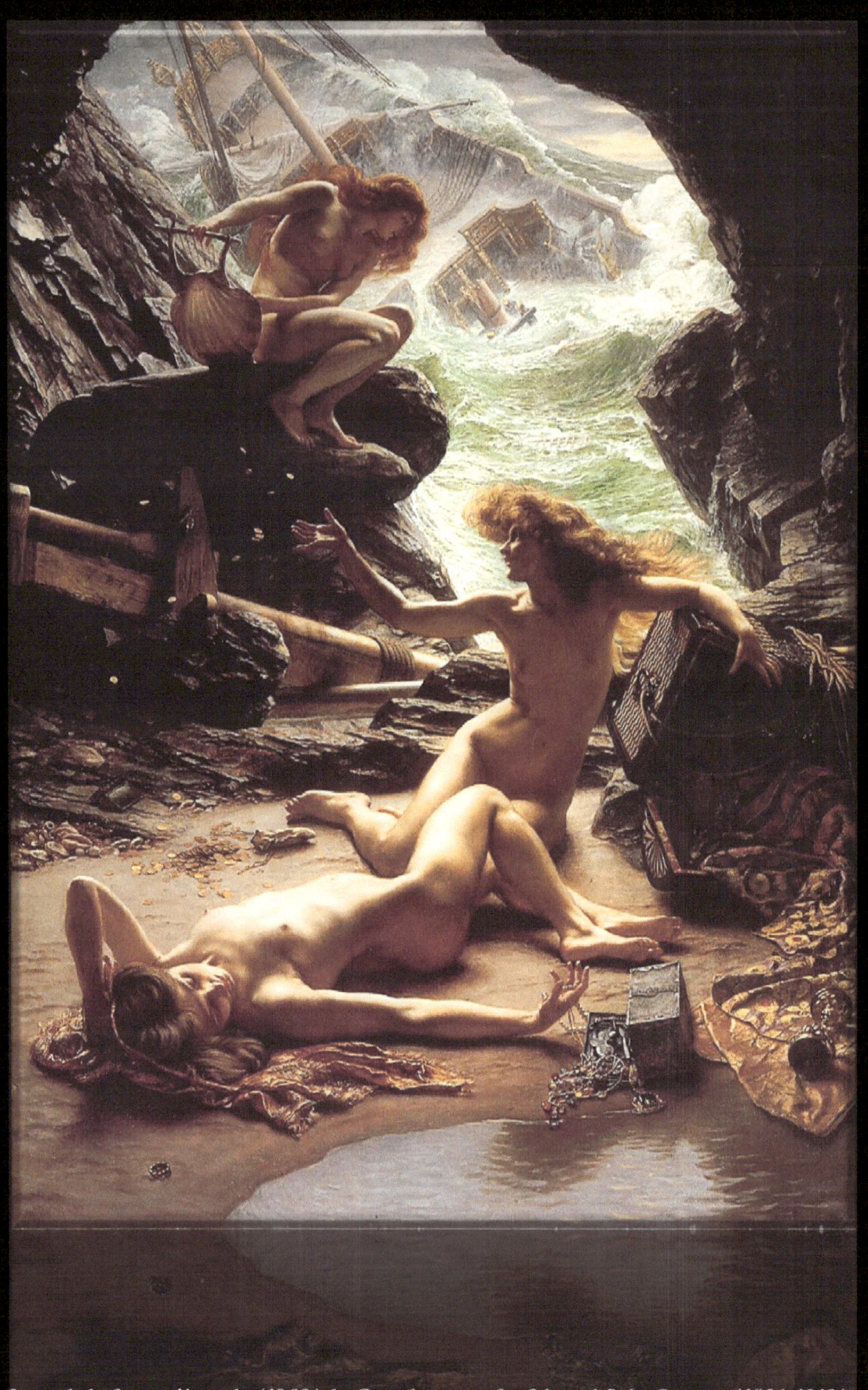

Cave of the Storm Nymphs (1903) by British painter Sir Edward John Poynter (1836-1919),

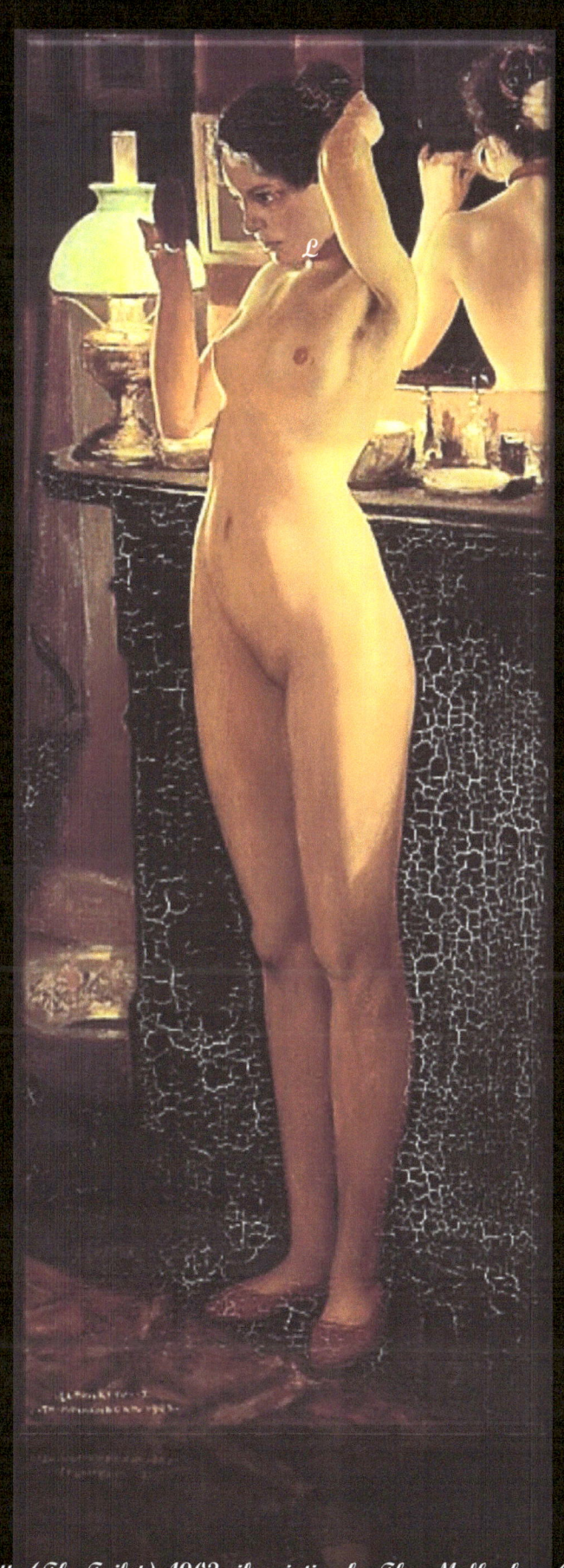

a Toilette (The Toilet), 1903 oil painting by Theo Molkenboer (1871-1920)

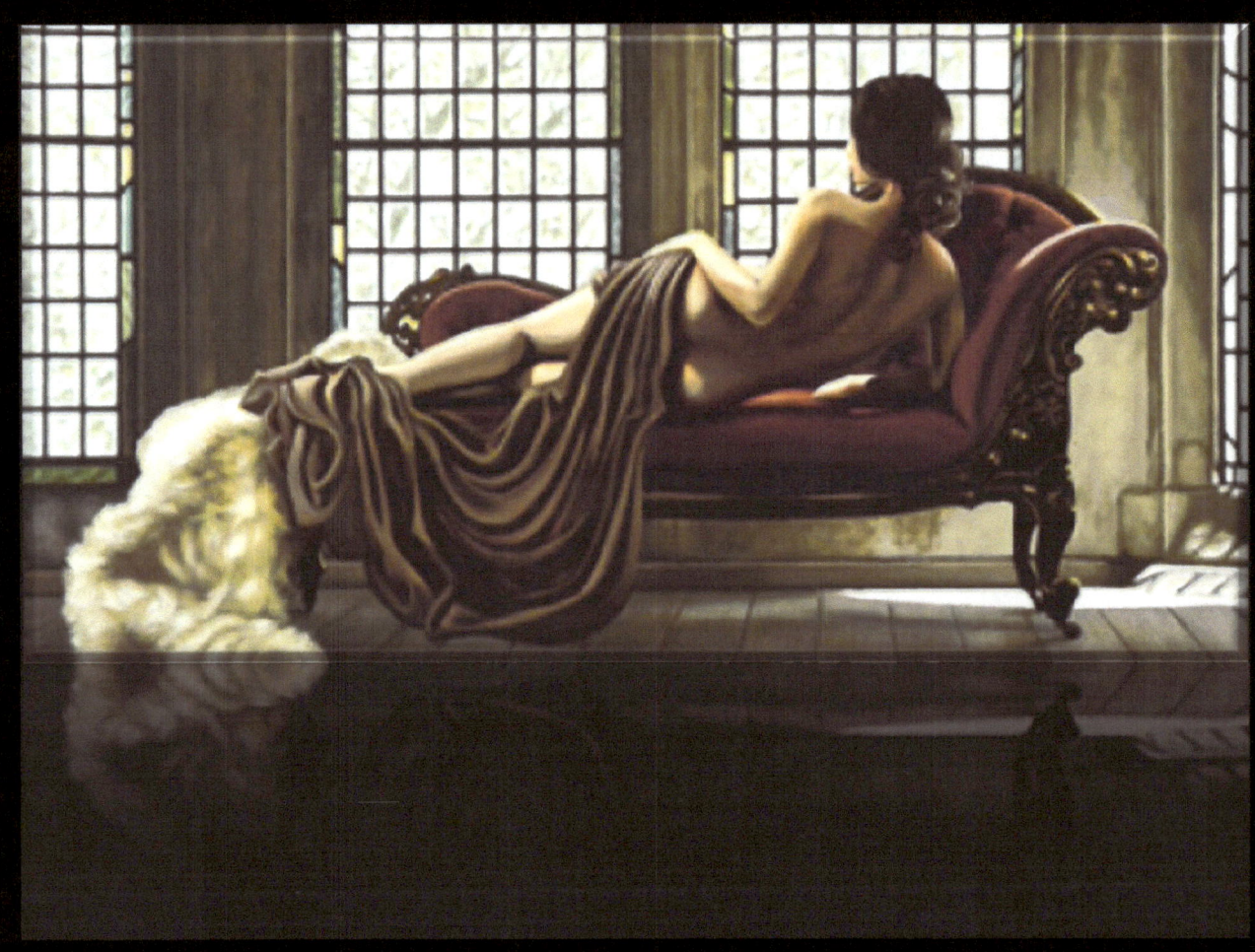

Golden Woman
Thomas Page

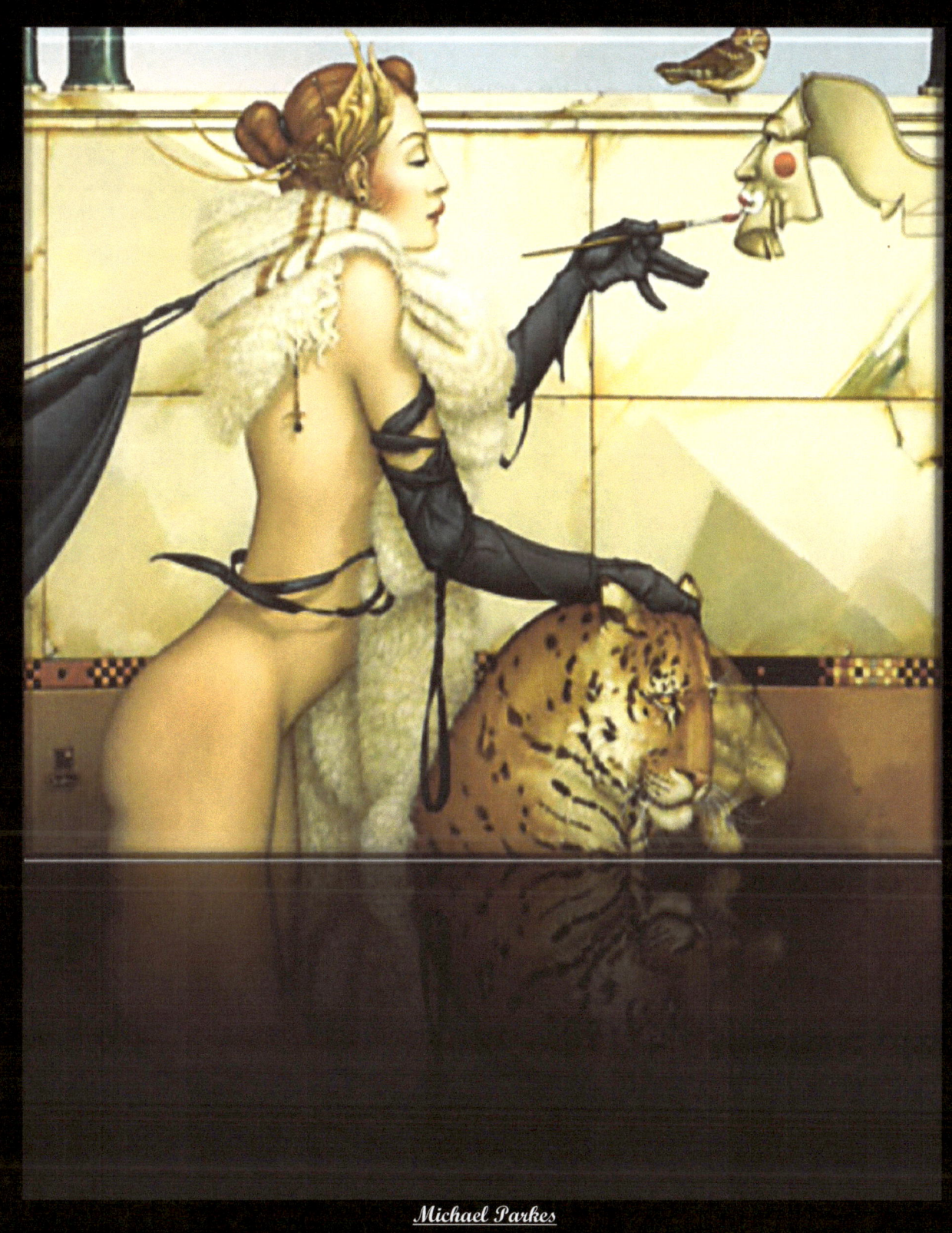

Michael Parkes
The Creation

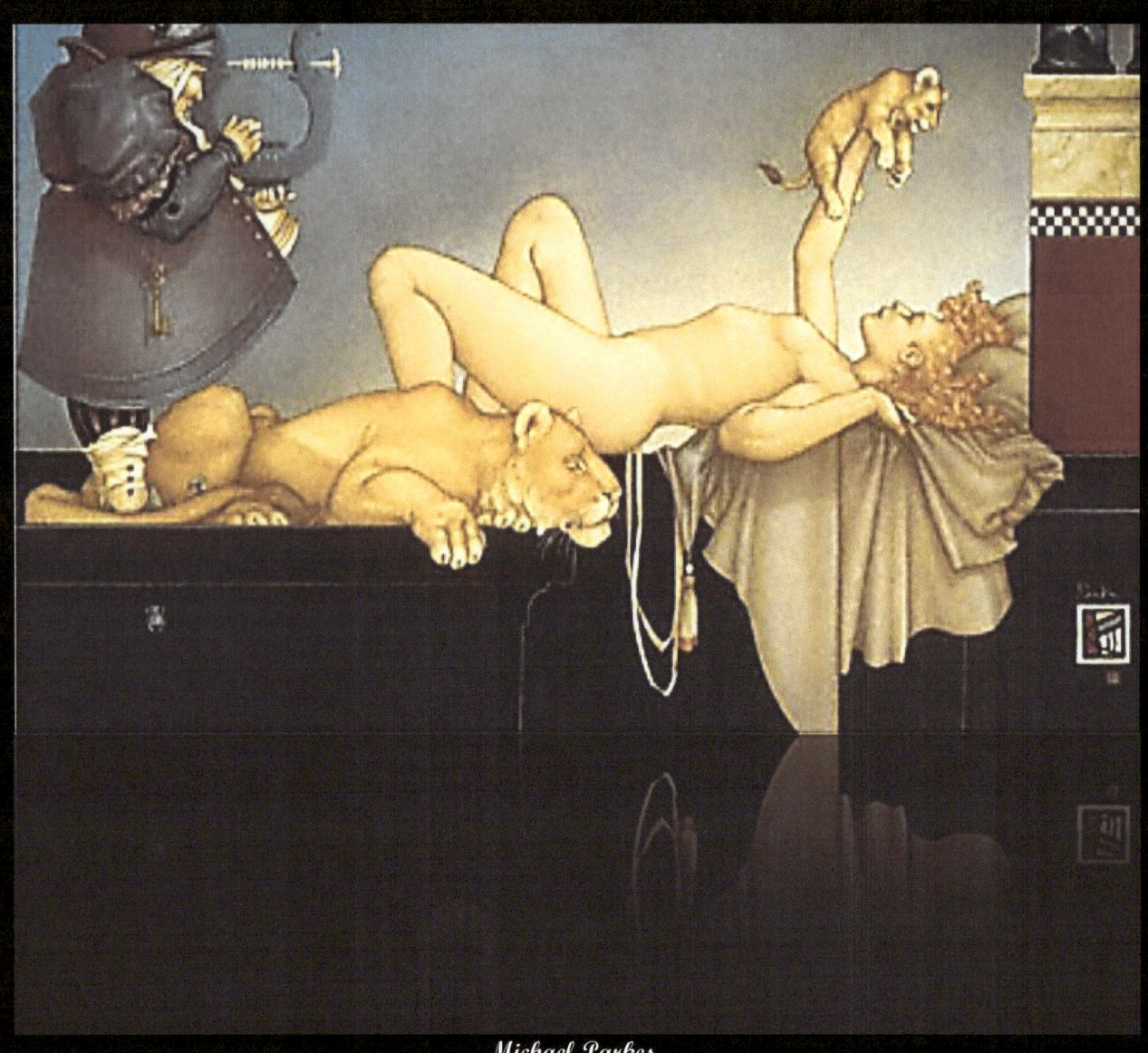

Michael Parkes
Dawn

Art L'Amour Sensuel

Showing the world the diversity in timeless art.

Collectors Edition,